GOOD GRIEF FOR NOW AND LATER

C Edward Mason

Good Grief For Now and Later by C Edward Mason
Published by Isabella Media Inc
270 Bellevue Ave #1002,
Newport RI 02840
www.IsabellaMedia.com

© 2022 Isabella Media Inc

All rights reserved. No portion of this book may be reproduced in any form without permission from the publisher, except as permitted by U.S. copyright law.
ISBN-13: 979-8-9862460-0-0

For permissions contact: requests@isabellamedia.com

Dedication

This book is being dedicated to the memory of

Deacon Dr. Herbert Goodman Jr. 1947–2019.

Dr. Goodman facilitated the Trinity United Church of Christ Emmaus Road Grief Counseling Ministry for nearly 30 years.

ACKNOWLEDEMENT

A special thanks to **James & Regina Spiller** for suggesting that I write this book while traveling with Sherri and me in Australia and New Zealand in 2012. It took seven years before I began writing, but it was all in God's timing to prepare me to tell the stories shared here.

Eric Lincoln Miller, 3iBooks Literary Agency, Reno, Nevada, for his consultation and guidance from the start to finish of this publication.

Carol Petersen Purroy, Author, Editor, and Publisher of A-Z Publishing, Reno, Nevada, edited this work and taught me plenty I did not know about being an author.

To the following who read the manuscript and gave critique and input for the book:
Donald R. Blanton, Andrea Brookins Brown, Thurman J. Chisholm, Jenny Dilts, Pamela J. Goodman, Renita Q. Ward and finally my Senior Pastor, **Rev. Dr. Otis Moss III.**

Aris Simpson for her photograph taken of me a few years before this book was written and
Rupert F. Graham Jr. for his video editing for the book promotion.

A special thanks to my wife Sherri, who not only was one who read the manuscript and gave her ideas and input, but also was my inspiration in every aspect from start to finish.

CONTENTS

Chapter 1 Different Funerals 1
- Arrangements Announced 2
- Short Funerals 4
- Long Funerals 5
- Absentee Funerals 6
- Double Eulogies 7
- Humorous Funerals 9

Chapter 2 It's Personal 11
- Crip's Wake 11
- My Mother 12
- My Brother 14
- Heaven Bound 18
- Cemetery Property 19
- Doctor Mother 20
- Suicide Chosen 21
- My Aunt 24
- Financial Impact 26

Chapter 3 Two Sides 29
- New Creation 30
- Father's Legacy 32
- Who's That? 34
- Games Played 35

Chapter 4 Shared Stories 39
- Quick Eulogy 39
- Wrong Scripture 40

- Soloist Found 41
- Goodbye Kiss 42
- Boat Rockin' 42
- Funeral Procession 43
- Comedian's Eulogy 44

Chapter 5 Unfamiliar Funerals 47
- African Funerals 47
- Religious Practices 49
- Other Beliefs 50
- Pet Funerals 52
- Children Funerals 54
- Quarantined Tears 57

Chapter 6 Spoken Words 61
- Son's Confession 62
- Match Making 64
- Grief Denial 65

Chapter 7 Life Celebrations 67
- Minister's Farewell 67
- Distinguished Service 70
- Posthumous Recognition 72
- Active Senior 72

Chapter 8 The Unexpected 75
- Distractions Judged 75
- Seeing Double 77
- Cold Distractions 77
- Funeral Directors 80
- Secret Shared 81
- Father's Grief 83
- Family Drama 84
- Left Behind 86
- Words Expressed 87

Chapter 9 Seasonal Sadness **91**
- Opening triggers 91
- Remembrance Services 92
- Coping Strategies 92

Chapter 10 The Burial **97**
- Prelude 97
- Late Arrival 98
- Military Burial 99
- Double Wide 101

The Epilogue **103**

Introduction

While in college, I gave serious thought to becoming a funeral director. I had been inspired by the work I did on a final exam speech I gave in Professor Solomon Baxter's Speech class. Professor Baxter was a sharp-dressed, middle-aged Jewish gentleman with a quirky sense of humor. I recall several times during the semester when he would correct a student's pronunciation of the word, 'often.' When one would mispronounce it, he would immediately say, "It's pronounced 'offin' – to rhyme with coffin." The final presentation for his class needed to include all the types of speeches we had studied that semester. The last had to be entertaining, informative, persuasive, explanatory, and motivational. It didn't take me long to develop my speech topic: The Work of a Funeral Director.

One of my mentors happened to be one of many funeral directors in Dayton, OH, where I spent my first year of college. I met with him and brainstormed how I could make this presentation. After a couple of meetings with him, I had all the ideas I needed to make this speech and guarantee me an excellent grade on the final. Little did I know the impact this speech would have on Professor Baxter, the students, and me.

The day of my final exam arrived. To enhance my presentation, I had borrowed an infant-sized casket from my mentor's funeral home and several items used in the funeral industry, including a trocar (the device used to remove bodily fluids from the deceased); eyelid caps (used to keep the eyelids of the departed closed); embalming fluid; and even sad organ music. After using all these visual and audio aids, my presentation was a hit with Professor Baxter. He asked me to do the same presentation for another class. I later learned from him what other students had to say about my presentation – comments like entertaining, morbid, scary, and informative. Yes, I got an A.

However, instead of pursuing that field and going on to a school of Mortuary Science, I chose a career that led me to work for 11 years with the Boy Scouts of America. Later, I worked 28 years in the financial services industry, from which I would retire. Much to my surprise, the work I did in that speech class in college years before would become an integral part of my writing this book to minister to those who mourn and grieve.

I figured there are hundreds of grief and mourning scenarios I could write about. However, I have narrowed them down to a little over fifty to cover a range of situations you may be facing now or sometime in the future.

Today, I average 60–75 funerals a year either as an officiant or as an attendee. Most people see nowhere close to that number annually. Since being an ordained deacon, this is one of the ways in which I have ministered to families in our church, a congregation of over 8,000. I have learned that many people don't want to talk about death, let alone deal with it on a personal level. Let's face it, we all must deal with it sooner or later.

The following chapters outline highlights of life lessons taught from the many funerals or bereavements in which I've been involved. I trust you will find information that will be a source of encouragement to you, your family, and any friends going through a time of grief. Although to most, it's a time of intense grieving and tears, some of these 'homegoing services' provide healing through the humor and inspiration involved in the celebration of the life, love, and legacy of someone who has passed away. Allow me to share my memoirs titled *Good Grief for Now and Later*.

Chapter 1

Different Funerals

"It doesn't matter how long you live, but how well you do it."

Dr. Martin Luther King Jr.

I have always felt that there is a difference between a funeral and a Homegoing celebration. Funerals are sad tearful and leave the mourners feeling hopeless. The service itself leaves you saying goodbye because you know you will never see that person again. On the other hand, the Homegoing service truly celebrates a life well-lived. The time you spend at that service has a much more celebratory atmosphere. It leaves you knowing in your heart that you will see that person again on the other side.

Why do most of us avoid talking about or dealing with the topic of death? It's probably because we don't understand death. We feel it's final, and we will never see the deceased again. People also do not want to deal with their mortality. Most people are scared of the end because it's the great unknown. It's easier for many not to think about it. Denial? Religion attempts to reassure us that death has no sting, but most people are not convinced. Grief and mourning are often used interchangeably today, but the two are different. I have learned this from experience. Grief is internal, while mourning is external. Grief refers to our feeling on the inside after we have lost a loved one. On the other hand, mourning is our public response to our loss and is manifest in taking the grief we feel on the inside and expressing it with tears, crying, and other forms of public display.

I have seen many types of emotions displayed in all the funerals and memorial services of which I have been a part for many years. There have been services where the mourning process has resulted in anger, crying, laughter, silence, verbal outbursts, and several other reactions. It is clear everybody grieves and mourns in their own way.

Anger is often the result of some experience when a loved one is taken away unexpectedly, such as by accident, gun violence, or murder. The anger is often displaced aggression due to the person(s) causing the accident, the person pulling the trigger, or the person who may have committed the murder. Death upon a sudden or prolonged illness, also seems to make God the target of anger. Sometimes people may experience anger, not directed at a person or deity, but rather at the situation itself. "I'm mad because I'm mad. How could this happen? It's so unfair." Crying is an emotion shared by most as they remember the life of the one who passed away, and that they will no longer be seen on this side of life. Laughter is sometimes the result of covering up tears, while silence is the other side of that cover-up. Regardless of who we are, we will mourn in one of these ways or more. Allow me to take you through numerous ways I have seen people handle bereavement, both at the public service and outside the service.

Arrangements Announced

Early in my life, the part of the newspaper I would always read was the obituary section. I guess I was enamored reading how people died in alphabetical order on the printed pages of the paper (my humor). Although newspaper obituaries are still available today, they are the more expensive way of making death announcements. If the person who has passed is much older and has not embraced technology, the newspaper announcement may work in some cases. In addition to the newspaper, taking the personal telephone directory or cell phone of your loved one and forming the traditional phone chain to spread the news still works. Over my lifetime, I have been notified of arrangements by a phone chain only once. At that single time, I had already known of the arrangements. In more recent years, group emails, group text messages, Facebook, and other social media posts have become the preferred and quickest ways to deliver the message to large groups of people.

Two years in a row, I learned of two different deaths after having sent out Christmas cards. One was from a former colleague who lived out of state, and another was from a friend who lived in our metro area. In both cases, we had been missed in the funeral notifications, and the spouses each sent a Christmas card back with a copy of their spouse's obituary, apologizing for not having informed us. It is understandable in this day and time to overlook someone when you are grieving and trying to make arrangements. If you miss getting the announcement to someone, don't beat yourself up about it, you have a lot on your plate.

End-of-life planning is essential in order to have your wishes made known before you pass. It saves your family one less thing to disagree about while arrangements are being made. *Cake* is a free website that makes it a little easier for anyone to document and share their wishes and decisions. The family will have enough on their minds after you have taken your last breath, so be thoughtful, do not procrastinate – help them with some of the decisions that need to be made. That way, there will be no second-guessing, and your loved ones will be able to say, "This is the way they wanted it."

Short Funerals

The shortest funeral I've attended lasted only 12 minutes. It was conducted at a funeral home by a deacon in the Catholic Church. This, by far, is not the norm when family and friends gather to say farewell to someone. This 12-minute funeral didn't give the small crowd assembled a chance to express any form of mourning. You could easily tell the eulogist was nervous and probably had minimal experience officiating at funerals. After these few unorthodox minutes and the sprinkling of the holy water, the assembled crowd was ushered out of the funeral home to the cemetery. I felt it was a sad and brief farewell to a man who had accomplished some great things in his life according to his obituary. A family can decide what can be said, what songs can be sung, or determine other rituals that may occur. But 12 minutes barely gives you time to get situated or comfortable. The average Protestant funeral seems to be about an hour. The order of service for most follows this same or similar order:

Procession of the family (Clergy reading Scriptures)

Invocation

Hymn of Consolation

Reading of Old Testament and New Testament Scripture

Ministry of Music

Tributes (generally 3–5 and limited to two minutes)

Resolutions read

Reading of obituary (Read either silently or by designated person)

Ministry of Music

Words of Comfort/Eulogy

Benediction

Recessional

Even with these listed items on a funeral program, these parts usually take more than a few minutes each.

I have always felt that funerals are for the living, not the dead. The funeral allows us some closure as we celebrate the person recently alive, and whose mortal remains now rest in the casket or urn. I also believe that something needs to be said about the deceased, not just some impersonal comments from a person who never knew the departed. The time to get a memorable message across to the grieving should not be so short to ignore the deceased totally, and not bring comfort to those attending. Nor should it be too long as to need an intermission, as was the longest funeral I ever experienced.

Long Funerals

In contrast to the shortest funeral I have witnessed, the longest one took eight hours and had an intermission … with refreshments. The deceased had been a pastor, and it occurred to me the service seemed less to honor his life than to resurrect him from death! It mostly followed the order of services listed in short funerals. Several things were added, and everything in the order of that service lasted way longer than in most homegoing services. There was a band, with numerous songs sung. Tributes came from at least 25 people who had no concept of the need for brevity. Had I not been so close to the family, I would have left after the intermission – the halfway point. Not only do long funerals prolong the mourning period but wear on the family and guests attending. This service started at noon and was not over until 8:00 p.m. It was dark by then, and going to the cemetery at night was not on the program. However, a burial service was scheduled for the following morning. Needless to say, after eight hours, I was through. I can only imagine how long the burial service lasted. Could it have been eight hours too? I never found out.

I believe there is probably a satisfying time medium for funerals. There needs to be a sufficient time for closure on that day, especially if there is a repast afterward where family and friends will gather for food and fellowship. Most importantly, the life of the loved one needs to be celebrated, whereby family and friends leave feeling uplifted and glad they had the chance to pay their last respects.

Absentee Funerals

Only once has this situation occurred in all the funerals I've attended. Our church had a memorial service for a 27-year-old young man the day before what would have been his 28th birthday. He had joined our congregation at the age of 11 but had never gotten involved other than attending an occasional Sunday service. My deacon team had been assigned to assist with this memorial service held in our chapel rather than the sanctuary like most funerals held at our church. There was no repast where light refreshments or a complete meal was served, just the memorial service at noon. I was running late that morning because I had been on a call with technical support people trying to troubleshoot my computer/printer problems.

I arrived at church at 12:05 p.m., knowing the services had just gotten underway. When I walked into the chapel, the only people there were our associate pastor, who was assigned to bring Words of Comfort, the organist, and six other deacons – nobody else. Here it was the day of the service, and nobody else was there – no family, no friends, no other church members, only the assembled participants. The minister explained she had reached out numerous times to the brother of the deceased, who had, a week earlier, consented to that date and time for the services. She had not heard back from the brother, who was not a member of our church. The minister went back to her office to try to reach the relative one last time.

This time the brother answered the call. He said he had left a message on her voicemail the day before. The day before was a Monday, the only day our church was closed. He proceeded to let the associate pastor know he had not been able to get the obituary programs, and we would have to reschedule the services. We are still waiting to hear back from that next of kin at this writing.

The dynamics of every family are different. Why this family chose not to handle the final arrangements for this loved one properly is beyond me.

I have discovered that when one dies young, there are generally many more people who attend the funeral compared to those who die at old age. Yet, that was not the case here. But not communicating the passing and arrangements to friends and family is still a mystery.

<u>Double Eulogies</u>

My wife and I attended the services of a young man who had once belonged to our church but had left several years before he passed away. The family chose to have a Saturday funeral. Hence, the service was held at a funeral home. Due to the multitude of activities held at our church on Saturdays, funerals are usually scheduled Tuesday through Friday. The young man's spouse as well as his mother – you could tell by their faces – had gone through a tearful time of mourning before arriving at the funeral home for the service. This funeral home had several chapels where funerals were held. The chapel we were in probably held 250 people. By 11:00 a.m., the chapel was filled, and the minister from the mother's church opened the service with prayer. Songs and scriptures followed his opening prayer.

After that, the minister asked for a second minister, listed on the program, to come forward. After a brief moment, no one responded, he called for resolutions and remarks. Several people came forward to read prepared resolutions, and another few spoke briefly about the deceased. After this part, the minister again asked if the minister listed in the program to do the Eulogy would please identify herself and come forward. Still, no one responded. A soloist was then called forward to sing. After she had sung and taken her seat, the minister who was to have given the words of comfort for the third time was asked to come forward. After a brief uncomfortable silence, the minister said, "Since the minister of the hour appears to be absent, allow me to speak a few words of comfort to this bereaved family." His message was brief, without any prior preparation – yet his words brought comfort to those assembled.

He then called for the funeral directors to open the casket for a final viewing before the benediction. As they ceremoniously lifted the lid from the coffin, the minister who was to have given the words of comfort finally showed up. While the organist played softly, the two ministers and the funeral home personnel conversed. The minister who had conducted the service until then introduced her. She took her place at the podium and apologized for her tardiness. It appeared her car's navigation system had taken her to another funeral home with the same name, in a community some 30 miles away.

Nonetheless, we listened to her prepared Words of Comfort. Like the first minister, who had delivered the first Eulogy, she was brief, and her oration also ministered to those still seated. Finally, after two messages, it was time to review the body, have the benediction and the recessional. Even with two eulogies, the visitation and the service lasted about two hours. No one seemed to mind.

Note: If you plan to attend a funeral, whether you're on the program or not, make sure you know where you're going so you can arrive on time and at the right place.

Humorous Funerals

I love comedy. Laughter is good for the soul. But continuous laughter at a funeral is not something I had experienced until one of our well-known church members passed away. If you'd belonged to our church for even a month, you'd have known her. With over 60 possible ministries, she was in everyone that would let her be involved. She would have joined the men's chorus and other men-only groups if their bylaws had allowed it.

I had worked with her in a couple of ministries for almost 15 years and knew her quite well. She was the only person who gave me a birthday card each year with two dollars in it. She lived her life to the fullest, and we all knew that her favorite meal was Popeye's chicken and Pepsi. She was the life of the party wherever she went and always took control, no matter what was going on. The last few years of her life, she threw a birthday party for herself in the summer. Indeed, having a birthday party is fine, but when your birthday is the week of Christmas, you wonder why she had a summer birthday party. As a child, she never had birthday parties since her birthday was during Christmas week. Any presents she got were usually in Christmas wrap. Therefore, she chose a time to celebrate when people would show up and bring *birthday* gifts.

She was an innate practical jokester with a unique sense of humor. Despite all her pranks and jokes, she had a love for the Lord and her church. Shortly before her passing, she called the church and stated, "I've got some good news and some bad news. The bad news is that I'm back in the hospital. The good news is, I'm not pregnant." Coming from a woman nearing her 71st birthday made this declaration hilarious.

A few weeks later, at her Homegoing celebration we learned that she had prepared her own service. She didn't want anyone to be sad and shed tears. She even instructed our pastor to bring on the comedy, and that he did. All those who gave remarks shared the fun stories of her life and kept a packed sanctuary in laughter. When our pastor finally got up to bring Words of Comfort, he became a stand-up comedian. One-liner after one-liner about her life kept those in attendance in constant laughter. I had never been to a funeral quite like it before, and none since – indeed a celebration of life and laughter no one there would soon forget.

Thoughts to ponder: What plans have you made for your passing that will help make things easier on your family and loved ones? Are they in writing? And does your family know where to find your written plans?

Chapter 2

It's Personal

"What we once enjoyed and deeply loved we can never lose, for all that we love deeply becomes part of us."

--Helen Keller

The first funeral I attended was as a four- or five-year-old boy. Our family took care of a man we called Crip. I don't know how old Crip was when he passed, but when you're a youthful four or five, everybody beyond 21 is old. I remember the visitation and our family going to the funeral home. This was the first time I saw someone displayed in a casket. Quite naturally, I was inquisitive. I asked my mother why Crip was lying here rather than at our house. Another series of questions followed. My father or mother answered each one there at the visitation. Being a nosey kid, I was tall enough to look at the foot of the casket. I lifted the silk material that hid the lower half of the body, and another question came to mind. "Why doesn't Crip have on shoes?" To that, my mother responded, "Enough with the questions!"

In the years that followed, I attended many family funerals.

Both of my parents passed away in the 1980s within three years of each other. Aunts, uncles, a brother, and many cousins on both sides of my family have all gone before me. I have been able to attend their services as a family member. As I reflect on each one, the main thing in common, other than the fact we were all related, was that it was a reunion time where we all would promise to get together at other times when the occasion would not be so sad. It wasn't until after my mother passed in 1986 did her side of the family start having reunions. The Blanton-Hawkins family reunions began to take place around the country every two or three years. The reunions allowed us time to get to know our growing family. At one of my last counts, my mother's side of our family had spread out from its Indiana and Kentucky beginnings to reside in 18 or 19 states. It's good for families to develop bonds and realize that getting together as often as possible, outside of funerals, allows you to see the three, four, or five generations that are part of the family tree. This, for many, as it did for me, develops an interest in one's family ancestry. It's always a good thing to know who your people are.

<u>My Mother</u>

My mother was the person who had the most significant impact on my life growing up. She was the perfect human being, but, as I got older, I learned she had her issues, just like the rest of us. She was the oldest sister; her personality and leadership carried over into her adult life. Our house was the go-to house for family and friends all the time. However, I later ascertained that my father was abusive. By the time I was 12 years old, my dad was arrested and later spent time behind bars. My mother divorced him and moved her three children still at home to Dayton, Ohio. We lived there until she remarried and moved back to our hometown. At the time, I was in my senior year of high school. My mother talked to my aunt and uncle about my living with them for my senior year. They agreed. I stayed in Dayton and lived with their children, my cousins, ages 10–17, becoming the 6th kid in their household.

My mother did not attend church but encouraged us to do so. Over my younger years, I talked to Mom on occasion about going to church with us. My mom told me as a PK (preacher's kid) – her father was a Methodist minister – she was forced to go to church. But my mom no longer saw the need to be involved in organized religion. Fast forward to my mid-30s: my mother's lung cancer had metastasized, and she was in hospice care.

In November of that year, I drove from Kansas City to Richmond to spend the weekend with her at the same hospital where I was born. After my arrival that Friday evening, hours went by with nurses, doctors, and other hospital types coming in and out of her room. I sat there with my stepfather that evening, looking forward to a few minutes alone with the woman who had brought me into this world. There was not a moment of privacy that I could talk with my mother about what mattered most, which was, where would she spend eternity? I drove my stepfather home, and I spent the night there. The following morning, after visiting hours began, I was in her room once again. My stepfather had some business to attend to, so I had come alone. That Saturday morning started as Friday night had ended – hospital personnel in and out of her room, for over an hour. I prayed, "Lord, I just need 20–30 minutes of privacy with my mom." Well, the Lord answered that prayer. Within minutes, all the traffic in and out of her room had stopped. I was able to talk with her privately, without somebody checking on her vitals, giving her pills, and the myriad of things that had been going on.

I asked her if she was prepared to go to Heaven. She answered, "I'm not sure." I let her know she *could* be sure and asked, "May I read a passage of scripture to you?" She responded in the affirmative.

I opened my Bible and read to her from Matthew 20:1–16. To paraphrase the passage, the landowner had hired workers for his vineyard, some in the morning at 9:00, more at noon, and the last hires at 3:00. He promised them all the same wage. They all were paid the same amount at the end of the day. But the ones he hired in the morning complained. Because they had worked longer, they thought they should be paid more. The landowner reminded them they all had agreed to the same wage, regardless of the number of hours worked.

I shared with my mother that God is like that landowner. He invites us all to receive the gift of eternal life if we accept him. Whether we come to him when we are young, middle-aged, or old, the reward is eternal life. I assured her it was not too late for her to decide upon eternal life. I asked her if she was ready to ask for forgiveness and invite God back into her life, to which she responded, Yes.

I then led her in a Salvation Prayer, after which tears rolled down both of our faces. I then affirmed, "You have now come home and are part of the family of God, with your reward being eternal life."

My mother had birthed me into the world physically, and now God had given me the chance to help birth her into spiritual eternity. We embraced. Moments later, the entourage of nurses, doctors, and miscellaneous personnel started making their way through her room one by one, just as before.

Less than two months later, on January 7th, Mama got her wings and went home to be with the Lord. I thank God that when we laid her to rest on January 11th, it was not Goodbye, but see you later.

My Brother

When my mother passed from the ravages of cancer, I learned a lesson that so many families experience that can genuinely divide them. After my dad passed away, I left my mother with a Document Location Record for her to complete. This two-page document allows one to write down the location of all one's essential records: wills, insurance policies, auto titles, mortgage deeds, safe deposit boxes, *et cetera*. When she passed away less than three years after Dad, I went home to help prepare for her funeral. I looked for this document location record and eventually found it – blank. It was a good thing I had written down the insurance company's name and policy numbers because we never found the policies either.

After her services, on the way home from Indiana to Kansas City, I had an appointment in Indianapolis to complete the claims paperwork on her two life insurance policies. After getting to the district office of the insurance company, I explained again we could not locate the policies but did have the policy numbers. They understood, and we completed the paperwork and returned home. A few days later, my oldest brother, who lived in Richmond, IN, our hometown, called me, stating the funeral director wanted to know when he would get his money. I told him that I had completed the paperwork in Indianapolis, and it would soon be mailed to him. Well, daily, for the next three weeks, my brother called to tell me the funeral director was still waiting on his money. Finally, I knew when the money had gotten to him because the phone calls had stopped. Calls between my oldest brother and me also stopped for 22 years. Oh, I would see him when I went home each year, but our phone calls had ended. The problem: he thought I was trying to get the money from our mother's insurance policies and leave him with the bill for the funeral. Nothing was further from the truth. Our lack of communication caused a split in our relationship for all those years.

Fast forward: 22 years later, I learned my brother was quite ill and given about a year to live. I decided to keep my black suit ready and wait till he passed away, then drive to my hometown for his funeral. But something inside me would not give me peace to wait. I decided I needed to visit my brother in the nursing home and try to make up for the 22-years we hadn't spoken, at least by phone. When I got to the nursing home, we started with small talk. It didn't take long for me to ask the question on my mind. My brother was nicknamed Sonny and I said, "Sonny, why didn't you ever call me after the insurance check arrived to pay the funeral home?" Macular degeneration had taken his sight. Uncontrolled diabetes had taken both legs. He cleared his throat and said, "You didn't call me either." For the first time in 22 years I felt the tears run down my cheeks as I realized I was just as guilty. We hugged and apologized for not communicating. We spent that weekend together in his nursing home room. My brother, a deacon in the Baptist Church, and I had time to share and try to make up for the last 22 years.

He asked me about my ministry as a deacon. That was a turning point in my life and probably the main reason for writing this book. I told him why I was not actively serving. After giving him my explanation, he said, "Once you are ordained a deacon, you're always a deacon." Those words weighed so heavily on me that, upon my return to Chicago, I could no longer deny my calling. Shortly after that, I went through my church's deacon-in-training program and was ordained a second time. Had it not been for my reconciliation with my brother, this book may never have been written, and I would not be serving as a deacon in my church.

Almost a year after our weekend together, my brother passed away. Days before his Homegoing service, I wrote a poem to honor his memory so I could read it at his services. These are the words that best described the man with whom I had not communicated for 22 years, as I should have:

Reflections on the Life of Baxter Eugene Mason

27,245 days was the time God gave him to live his life and abound,
spending all his years in the city of Richmond on every side of town,
this was where he called home, though some family members
had moved away,
Working at Wayne Works, manufacturing buses,
is how he spent his workdays.

Early in life he developed a passion for baseball,
football, and other games
he would spend hours on games and knew all
the players by position and name,

but when it came time to work, he put sports
aside and took his clue from our dad,
Whatever the job called for, he gave it everything he had.

Sonny, as we called him, had a good memory for all dates,
be it the year 1953 or late in 1968,
he would argue with you the facts concerning the events of this time,
and it was always difficult to win an argument
against his photographic mind.

Many people tune in to the television news to watch the weather,
but when Baxter came around, his forecast
is what you would always gather,
playing checkers was another pastime, in which he could not be beat,
he was always three moves ahead and looking
for the next challenger to defeat.

Old cars kept him moving, he'd be all over town,
when he would stop by your house, he never had long to stick around,
hospitals and nursing homes were always on his mind,
visiting and praying with the sick and shut-in and giving of his time.

On Sundays he would don a sports coat and tie,
but when not at Mt. Olive Church, bib overalls were his best buy,
Deacon Mason often led devotions before he was laid up,
and he could often be heard asking the congregation,
"Church, are you fired up?"

Our brother and dad both were private,
neither talking much about self,
they even both suffered somewhat quietly,
when they fell into ill health,
even though their bodies were both succumbing
to the ravages of disease,
if you stopped in their room to visit, their talk
of home-going would put you at ease.

Yes, we will miss Sonny and the memories he leaves to cherish
for all the family loved him and his spirit will never perish,
to us he was a daddy, grandpa, brother, uncle, cousin, and friend,
and because of this, Deacon Baxter Eugene
Mason's memory will never end.

It was reassuring that I had reconciled with my brother. When his passing finally came, it assured me I had done the right thing. I had experienced too many people who were going through a period of grief and mourning who would say words like "Had only we made up before this happened," or, "I wish I could have told him what I felt," or, "If I had only not put off going by to see her," *et cetera*.

It may not be too late to do what is in your heart right now. Don't put it off any longer.

Heaven Bound

Growing up in Indiana, I saw a billboard every day on my way to school. The sign simply stated, "Everybody wants to go to Heaven, but nobody wants to die to get there." As a youngster, I often pondered those words. Even today, as an adult, the same is true. At a funeral I attended not long ago, the minister summed up our desire to go to heaven like this: "Death is the vehicle that will get you to heaven. There are three modes of transportation to take us there, and they all begin with the letter A.

The first A is for *Age*. Some of us will live to old age and get transported due to natural causes of aging.

The second A is for *Accident*. Whether the accident is from an automobile, plane, train, or other means of accidental death, those too will transport us to heaven.

The third A represents an *Agent of death*. Many have succumbed to diseases, from cancer to heart disease, and a myriad of illnesses and diseases in between, all of which will transport us from earth to heaven.

With each passing day, we all get closer to our final mode of transportation from this life.

Cemetery Property

Shortly after the funeral of a family member, I recall getting a letter in the mail about pre-need arrangements and purchasing cemetery plots. I returned the postcard included in this letter, and a short time later a salesman called to explain the offer to which I had responded. His presentation was very dignified and professional. I was so convinced of the need and cost savings that my wife and I purchased cemetery plots in advance of our need to do so. Although I was employed already, I inquired of the older gentleman who had entered our home if this could be done on a part-time basis, to which he responded yes. I went to an interview. About a week later, I was hired and trained to sell 'heavenly real estate' part-time. The leads were supplied each week from postcard responses, just as I had done. I had 3–4 appointments each week. My closing rate was extremely high and, for a little more than a year, I made good supplementary income. Even more important than the income was the fact I was providing a much-needed service and product that would save people money. In my mind, buying the plots before the need arose was the way to go. Too many people, I had learned, waited till a death had occurred in the family, upon which they would have to pay higher prices and deal with all the decisions that must be made during this critical time of grief and mourning. Planning for one's death just made sense to me. Someone dies every day, and everyone dies someday. So why not save your family money and time and get it done before the need occurs? Some years later, with my second wife, I went one step further: we sat down with our funeral director friend and pre-planned both our funerals.

Doctor Mother

My mother-in-law got her Ph.D. at the age of 65. How proud she was of her accomplishment! From that day on she was addressed as Dr. Miller in everything she said and did. Her voice mail at home, her return address mailing labels, her stationary, all new introductions would let you know she was *Dr.* Miller. Some months later, my wife Sherri and I visited her at her home. I was in a jovial mood that day. At one point in our conversation, I asked her, "Mother, now that you have your Ph.D. do you want me to refer to you as Dr. Mother?" Giving me a slight smile, she responded, "No, *Mother* will do just fine."

Nearly thirteen years later, my wife and I moved through four months near the end of her mother's life. That November, Dr. Miller had been diagnosed with an inoperable brain tumor. It had a long medical name that seemed like 40 letters. For the next four months, we were back and forth to the hospital, then the nursing home, and finally home hospice care as the end neared. Watching my wife's mother slip away slowly prompted a feeling of helplessness.

Just as much of an experience was watching all the family interactions … or lack of them. My wife had been adopted by her great aunt and uncle while a baby. As a young adult she tried to establish a relationship with her birth mother. Some years they got along, and some they did not. It took me a while to learn the family dynamics, but after a few years of marriage, I became aware how both sides of their relationship caused sadness and pain. They tried to work out their differences, sometimes with success and other times not. But during the final four months of her life, other family members became involved in various ways. However, family dynamics being what they were, there was family unrest and agitation that persisted right up until the day of the funeral.

As a husband, I needed to support my wife as much as possible. My mother-in-law grew up in Youngstown, Ohio. Her funeral was held in her home church. This decision was made by my wife's half-brother.

He wanted to control the guest list at his mother's funeral. He reasoned that 'undesirables' would not attend if it had been held at his mother's home church, more than four hours away. I've discovered that people often become meaner than usual during these times.

After the Homegoing services for my mother-in-law had concluded and we traveled back home, my wife was overwhelmed by the cards she had received from our church members, as well as other friends and family. Many of the cards contained contributions of money, which was unexpected. This was my first experience with these contributions, but it appears to be a common practice.

If a person can do so, I'm sure the money goes a lot further and can be used by the family far better than flowers. Making contributions in the deceased's name to whatever charity the family requests is also a preferred way to 'pay your respects.'

It's often said, give people flowers while they can smell them. I agree, that is a much more preferable way to let someone know you care.

Suicide Chosen

People die every day of many different causes. One of the most challenging reasons for death I have experienced is when one takes their own life. Regardless of the method of suicide, it impacts family and friends alike. It's said that suicide is a permanent solution to a temporary problem. Mental disorders, including depression, bipolar disorder, schizophrenia, personality disorders, anxiety disorders, and substance abuse – including alcoholism and the use of benzodiazepines – are risk factors. Some suicides are impulsive acts due to stress, such as financial difficulties, relationship problems such as breakups, or bullying. Suicides among young people continue to be a severe problem. Suicide is the second leading cause of death for children, adolescents, and young adults aged 15-to-24-year-olds. Those of all ages who have previously attempted suicide are at a higher risk for future attempts.

Statistics show that a note accompanied less than 30% of suicides. The first person I knew who died by suicide was a doctor who had been an active member of the first church I belonged to in Kansas City. We had worked together on a few committees during the first few years of my membership at that church, whose membership was about 500. I thought I had become well acquainted with him until there was a period when he stopped coming to church. I reached out to him, but we never managed to connect. One day, our pastor asked me to see him in his office. After taking a seat, my pastor asked, "Do you know of any reason Doc stopped coming to church and being active in ministry?" I answered, "No, I don't." The following statement from the pastor shocked me to the core. He had visited Doc at the hospital. One of the reasons Doc gave for dropping out of church activities was me. He told Pastor, "I dropped out of church activities because of Ed. Ever since Ed became a member and got involved in so much at our church, there's no longer anything for me to do." Pastor assured me this was only an excuse. The next thing Pastor shared with me was even more of a shock.

Doc had attempted suicide. Questions raced through my mind. #1: Why would a successful doctor with a wife and two small children want to take his life? I left the pastor's office vowing to pray for Doc and his family, as did several other members with whom Pastor had shared this information.

Many weeks went by before we got the news that Doc had again attempted suicide, this time successfully. My first reaction was a deep sense of sadness for his family, followed shortly after that by guilt. The first question I asked myself was, "What could I have done to perhaps prevent Doc from ending his life?" After talking to my pastor, he again reassured me the issue was much more profound, and there was probably nothing I could have done to change the outcome.

My wife and I both attended Doc's funeral. We greeted the grieving family briefly and took our seats as the services were about to start. Every seat was filled in the 250-seat sanctuary. For one of the first times in a lifetime of funeral attendance, I cannot remember much that happened after Doc's casket was closed.

A few months went by before I got a call from one of our members, who was also one of my financial planning clients. She let me know Doc's widow needed financial planning services. I indicated I felt uncomfortable talking with her because of my closeness to the family and the grieving I was still going through. My client, who was also a very close personal friend of our family, said, "I understand how you must feel, but Doc's widow needs your help now. She wants the financial counseling of someone she can trust, and that's you." Finally, a couple of days later, I reached out to the widow, making an appointment. Over a few weeks and three different meetings, from the insurance proceeds, I was able to help her implement a financial plan that gave her the monthly income she needed, investments for her future, and educational funds for her two small sons.

Although Doc, for whatever reason, felt the need to end his own life, the bright side was the fact I was a trusted friend and financial professional with whom his widow found confidence. With her confiding in me, together, we were able to begin putting the pieces of her family's life back together.

Many can say they are 'suicide survivors' due to losing a loved one in this manner. While there is no easy way to grieve, it may be helpful to seek resources for those who have lost someone to suicide or get involved in a grief support group. If you were close to the person who ended their own life, it's common to experience shock, denial, guilt, sadness, anger, isolation, and other mixed emotions. You may never get over the loss of this loved one, but you can get through it. The following suggestions may help you cope and heal in the weeks and months ahead:

1. **Seek Support**: Reach out to friends, family members, mental health counselors, or spiritual advisors who can be there to help you through these times.

2. **Be Patient:** You may be feeling a range of emotions. Take time to heal; do not rush into making major decisions. Limit time with people who may be harmful.

3. **Stay Present**: Take things one day at a time. Journaling may help; try relaxing and stay as positive as you can by reading uplifting material and listening to uplifting music.

4. **Express Yourself**: It's okay to tell others how you're feeling. Or if you choose to maintain your feelings privately, that may work also. Prayer and meditation are also ways to express yourself and seek inner peace.

5. **Take Care of Yourself**: Eat as well as you can, exercise daily, and avoid escaping into alcohol or drugs as a way to sedate yourself. This is a highly stressful time, and in the midst of it, one can experience (temporary) memory loss, inability to sleep, and inability to concentrate. It's advised that a to-do list, or setting reminders on your smartphones, *et cetera* be made daily for everyday tasks and appointments.

My Aunt

My mother was from a family of five: one male and four females. I have fond memories of each of my mother's siblings. One, in particular, was my Aunt Juanita. Growing up, she was the least healthy of all five, yet she outlived them all. In the latter years of her life, she was diagnosed with Alzheimer's. She ultimately was admitted to a nursing home as a resident of the Alzheimer's unit. During her final three or four years, my wife and I traveled from the Chicagoland area to Richmond, IN, to visit her. On one such occasion, we arrived but could not find Aunt Juanita. We looked over the entire Alzheimer's unit and the rest of the nursing home, but after 30 minutes, we had yet to locate her. We returned to her room, and as we entered, we heard noises from inside her closet. When we opened the door, there was Aunt Juanita frantically looking for something. When I asked her what she was looking for, she replied, "I don't remember, but when I find it, I'll let you know what it is." My wife and I just smiled, looked at one another, and led Aunt Juanita to the atrium area so we could sit and talk.

If you have ever had a family member with Alzheimer's, you can understand how this disease takes away memory. My aunt could remember things from her childhood nearly ninety years earlier, but could not remember what she had for breakfast two hours before. My aunt would always remind us that she was the least healthy of her siblings, yet she had outlived them all.

The last time my wife and I were to see Aunt Juanita alive would be to celebrate her 90th birthday. We left Chicago on that February morning with clear skies. We encountered a major snowstorm when we reached Crown Point, IN. The drive to my hometown, which took about four hours in good weather, was doubled that day. Although the drive was something I never want to experience again, at least we were able to see Aunt Juanita one last time. Two months later, she passed away. We attended her services, along with a number of our relatives and friends.

One thing that was somewhat humorous to me was the letter the nursing home sent. It was a very kind letter presenting my aunt as a model resident. That, we knew, was not true. There had been many times my brother Lawrence who was handling her affairs, called to tell me he had to head out to the nursing home to keep them from throwing Aunt Juanita out. She sometimes had an altercation with one of the other residents, cussed somebody out, or acted out in some different ways. A model resident, she was not! However, the services went well, and we still have a copy of the DVD with the inspiring music played during her visitation. Although she may have forgotten us toward the end, she will live on forever in our memories.

For those who have a loved one suffering from Alzheimer's today, I recommend you watch the movie, *Still Alice*. It's a drama produced in 2014 about a renowned linguistics professor at Columbia University.

The professor, named Dr. Alice Howland (played by Julianne Moore), comes face to face with a diagnosis of early-onset Alzheimer's. As the once-vibrant woman struggles to hang on to her sense of self, Alice's three grown children watch helplessly as their mother disappears into her 'own world' more and more as each day passes. By the end of the movie, the professor could not even find her way to the bathroom in her own home.

When my wife and I saw this movie, the theater in which we saw it was packed. We theatergoers made our exit in total silence. I believe we were all digesting the reality of what we had just witnessed on the big screen and how it could impact us.

If you lose a loved one to this dread disease, focus on your good memories of before their time of suffering this illness. Sure, you will miss them, but hold onto the positive, happy memories.

Financial Impact

One of the first times I learned how costly death could be was when my Uncle Alex died in the early seventies. He was married to my mother's sister, Christella, his second wife. I'd lived with Uncle Alex and Aunt Christella during my senior year of high school. Both were highly intelligent people who handled their family affairs well; or so I thought. After Uncle Alex's death, I learned he had never changed the beneficiary on his life insurance policies although he'd been married to his second wife for over twenty years! Hence, his first wife was the one who filed the insurance claims and received the payouts of these policies, not my aunt to whom he had been married longer. And he was the father of two of her five children. I remember talking to her on the phone on several occasions after he died. The financial impact of this always came up. However, she still held on to her faith that God would somehow provide for her financial needs. She struggled for some time after Uncle Alex's passing, but a couple of years later, she bought what proved to be a winning Ohio lottery ticket. She chose to receive about $50,000 each year from the proceeds. The loss of Uncle Alex's income was more than replaced and lasted her the remainder of her life. Financial hardship for the survivor(s) is not unheard of. Unfortunately, not everybody who suffers financially at the death of a loved one, especially a spouse, can count on winning a lottery. We all know we will die someday. The time to begin preparing for that is while we are still alive. Having an updated, current life insurance policy with the correctly-designated beneficiary is crucial. In addition, for married couples, at minimum, some estate planning should be done that includes individual wills. Couples who are not legally married should have an irrevocable living trust in place that indicates the beneficiaries of all shared assets. Protect your loved ones financially by making these decisions while you are still of sound mind.

Thoughts to Ponder:

- *Who in your family or circle of friendships do you need to be reconciled with, or have an end-of-life conversation with?*

- *Someone you know who has Alzheimer's. Make a list of all the attributes they exhibited before the memory loss began and think about that part of their life,* not *the loss.*

- *Are your insurance policies current?*

- *Will your heirs know where to find important documents?*

Chapter 3

Two Sides

"Life is for living. Death is for the dead. Let life be like music and death a note unsaid."

Langston Hughes

Have you been to a funeral, only to wonder who was being eulogized? I have experienced this phenomenon on several occasions. I have found a few reasons that may explain why the eulogy appears to be for someone you did not know.

The first reason I have found is that the clergy or person giving the message did not know the deceased and either made up things that were not relevant to that person, or they talked about anything *except* the dearly departed. If one is asked to deliver words of comfort to a grieving family, it helps if the one doing it takes time to meet with the family to get more relevant information about the person for whom they are sharing. It's also a good idea to write your memoirs. That will give the eulogist plenty of material to share about your life.

Secondly, I have found that we all have at least two sides, our public self and our private self, that fewer people know unless they are very close. The deceased may have had a work or business persona familiar to their colleagues and other work associates. Perhaps, a side of that person was only revealed around people with whom they socialized. Another side may have been seen by those with whom they attended religious services and related activities. Even further, there may have been a complete change in the person's belief system or lifestyle that you knew nothing about because you had not been in touch with them since such dramatic differences had come about in their life. I believe most of us do not know how others perceive us. And we may be unfamiliar with many of the quirks of even those we are close to.

New Creation

Several funerals in which I have been involved will exemplify these truisms. The first one was for a guy I knew who had been married, had two children, and had once been an active attendee at our church. Something happened in this guy's life that sent him on a downward spiral. He got involved in drugs, became abusive to his wife, and was later sent to prison for some offense of which I'm not aware. That was the last I saw of him until I learned of his death about fifteen years later. My wife and I decided to attend his funeral to pay our last respects. There was some mystery around his latter days. Before getting to the church where the funeral was held, my wife and I talked about our remembrances of him. We had more questions than answers before getting to the services. How did he pass away at the young age of 50? Did he die while he was incarcerated? Did he ever get his life back together after leaving the church? We also wondered whom he had known at this large suburban church where his services were held.

After entering the church and signing the guestbook, we headed to the front to view the body. He indeed looked like we remembered him from years before, only heavier. We doubted if we would see his ex-wife, to whom he had been so violent, but we felt his son and daughter, now in their teenage years, would be there. We found a seat in the crowded sanctuary and waited to see if we could see family to offer our condolences. It was not until the beginning of the service that we saw his daughter walk in and take a seat. It was the usual order of service that we were very accustomed to.

We had given our church's Resolution (a tribute to the deceased) to one of the ministers after we arrived. We were waiting for the time in the service it would be read – we, together with other members of our church, could stand, if asked, as it was read. Three people gave tributes, but they all seemed to be about someone other than the man we had known. While sitting there, I surmised that some significant changes had occurred in this man's life. We hadn't a clue. It wasn't until the minister got up to give his Words of Comfort that I realized why God wanted me to be there.

As the minister began, he read the scripture from 2 Corinthians 5:17 that read: *"Therefore if any man be in Christ, he is a new creature; old things are passed away; behold, all things are become new."* He stated that many knew the deceased from years ago when he was a vile and wretched man. However, that was not going to be the focus of his message. He said we all, like the deceased, have a past, but the focus was now on the new man he had become. He asked those who knew the new creation God had changed this man into to stand. Probably over 75% of those in attendance stood to their feet amid loud applause. While the pastor delivered his Eulogy, the questions my wife and I had had were all answered. He had become a different man while in prison. Because of my work in prison ministry, my ears were open. For a number of years, prison ministry members had been sharing the Gospel with this man and invited him to worship services at the prison.

This prodigal son had returned to the Lord after being in a reprobate state for several years. After getting out of prison, he was re-baptized and joined the church now holding his funeral. The pastor shared many stories of this converted man whom most of those in the church only knew after his conversion. Through his testimonies shared over two previous years, they had learned of his past and could not believe he had been as deplorable as he had shared.

That service helped me in two ways. First, it allowed me to know this man's ending was far better than his beginning. We celebrated the changed life of one on a path to destruction and now a new creation in Christ – ready for Heaven. Secondly, it renewed my faith in our prison ministries' work in penitentiaries all across the country. Our ministry's outreach is to six penal institutions at which we provide programs and services to those men, women and even juveniles behind bars. My commitment to it, as stated by Jesus in Matthew 25:36, *"...when I was in prison ye came to visit me,"* was reaffirmed that day. We are still called today to minister to the least of those forgotten and incarcerated.

Father's Legacy

At another Homegoing celebration we attended, I knew both sides of the deceased. I had known this brother for about 20 years and had worked with him on various projects. Unlike the man who had returned to the Lord before he died, this brother had held several high-profile positions in the church and community, both locally and nationally. I knew his business and political side, which garnered him many awards and citations. But I also knew about his personal life – his first marriage had ended in a bitter divorce, leaving two children (now grown) who never got to know their father, as they did their stepfather raised them.

There was a larger than usual crowd that day for the funeral. Everything seemed to run smoothly as the celebration of his life took place. The scriptures that were read, the songs sung, the tributes shared by five people who knew the deceased best were all in good taste. Even his son, who had never had a good relationship with his father, gave complimentary remarks though he barely knew his father. Our senior pastor shared a touching story of two brothers named Life and Death: The father had given the brother named Life a box. The brother named

Death was always trying to see what was inside. Each day, Life would rise, look into the box and then put it away. Years later, after Life had looked into the box as he did daily, he failed to put it away. Death found the box and took it. When Life discovered his box was missing, he went to his father. His father said, Death has taken your box, but before he could take its treasures, I removed them, and now Death only has an empty box.

The Eulogy was given by our Pastor Emeritus, who took his scripture from 1Samuel 16:7 and titled it "What God Sees." He went on to compare the life of the deceased with King David. This king, a man after God's own heart, was a great king but not a great father. After the service was over, the funeral procession to the cemetery began. I usually do not go to the cemetery, but this one, I did. I knew the family well and was close to the man's ex-wife, son, and daughter. After the <u>burial,</u> the repast was held about a half-hour from the cemetery. Upon arrival at the banquet facility, parking was a challenge, and inside was a full house of hungry people. After almost two hours, my wife and I decided it was time to head home, another 45-minute drive. Needless to say, when we got home, it was 6:00, and we were tired. We both thought this had brought closure to the life and legacy of this brother. A week later, we were surprised to learn what went on behind the scenes.

We were gathered at the home of the deceased's first wife, the mother of his son and daughter. Four couples had gathered for pizza, fellowship, and discussion about a movie we all had watched. Little did we know the ex-wife and daughter needed to share what they had experienced through this ongoing ordeal. We learned that the deceased had no life insurance to leave a financial legacy, let alone for burial expenses. The 24 hours following his death was met with bitterness, confusion, and shock, all of which did nothing to bring a family together. The repast, catered by a family member who was the proprietor of the banquet facility, was understood to be a donation. However, a few days later, the relative asked the children who would pay for the repast. Some gift, right?

Funerals do create an unexpected expense. Planning for that day should be the responsibility of the one who will be leaving a memory. Ignoring the inevitable and leaving it up to the survivors to reach out to friends, employers, and whoever else wants to be generous at this time should be avoided. The lack of money at this time of grief only makes the mourning burden that much greater.

Who's That?

The aunt of a friend of our family had passed away. My wife had told me about this lady, whom I had never met. During the services at her church, a sizable number of people had gathered. My wife had told me how mean this lady had been, and the unnecessarily cruel things she had been known to say. Nobody could escape her sharp tongue – what came up came out. She didn't care whom she offended.

The members of her church had nothing but flowery words to describe her. Each had stated qualities that truly made her appear equal to Mother Teresa. After the remarks went on for some twenty minutes by about five fellow church members, one of her nephews spoke up in a voice that could be heard by those sitting near, "Who in the hell are they talking about?"

Trying to enhance the image of the deceased usually does not go over well with those who really knew the person. But perhaps that might be a facet of the departed those eulogizers actually knew. Usually, family and friends are the ones who can really tell you who that person was, though even they may not be willing to tell it like it is at the funeral. This reminds me of the story of a man who went to a minister and offered him money to say good things about his brother, who had died in prison. On the day of the funeral, the minister rendered his eulogy and stated the deceased had been a thief, a violent man, a womanizer, and numerous other adjectives to describe the horrible things he had done. But, then the minister said, "Compared to his brother, he was a saint." People truly write their own eulogy by the lives they live.

Games Played

If you know the true me, you know a side of me that mere acquaintances may not see. I must confess, I am an incredibly competitive person when it comes to games. My three favorites are *Bid Whist* (a card game comparable to Bridge), *Scattergories* (a board game), and *Scrabble* (a word game). I started playing *Bid Whist* back in high school. I remember meeting a senior, like me, at Roosevelt High School, who in five years would become my first wife – she walked into a classroom where three classmates and I were playing *Bid Whist* during our free period.

My love of *Scattergories* began in 2007 when my sister Dorothy and her two daughters, Aisha, Marissa, and my daughter, Ajay spent a week with us that November. After Dorothy introduced us to this new game, we played it every day during their stay. And ever since then, there is not a month that goes by that we do not find time to play with other family members and friends. Two of our prayer partner friends, Andrea and Norval, are also quite competitive – their major goal when we play is to beat me at *Scattergories*.

I don't know exactly when I began to like *Scrabble*, but it was in 2011. I was laid up from a car accident and my sister introduced me to an electronic version of the game called *Words with Friends*, which could be played on a smartphone, iPad or computer. It became a pastime during my four months of physical therapy, in addition to reading and television.

But *Words with Friends* is the game I want to focus on. It gave me time to minister to a fellow church member during his extended illness. After starting to play, initially, I quickly added friends from my Facebook family, church, former colleagues, and others. A few years into my playing with up to 50 people and games during any given day, I reconnected with my Spanish teacher from my senior year at Roosevelt High. I recall my daughter Ajay asking me, "Do you have teachers who are still alive?" To this, I replied, "Yes, my high school

Spanish teacher is only four years and two months older than I am. Her first year of teaching was my senior year. We often play a game in Spanish and one in English." Out of the more than 50 friends I play with, the person who impacted my playing the most was one of our church's ushers named Joseph. I had ushered with Joseph during my years as an usher, but it wasn't until I began to actively serve as a deacon that I really got to know Joseph. He also served faithfully at funerals at our church. The ushers who can serve weekday funerals are called our Celebration of Life Team. Joseph was one we could always count on.

It wasn't until his long-term illness that I really came to know him. I was assigned to visit him in the hospital. It was there that I discovered his love for Words with Friends as well. We began to play, week after week. He always made time for his next move between his doctor visits, VA hospital stays, and rehab trips. If two days went by without him playing, I would text or call him to see how he was doing. After almost two years of playing with Joseph, the doctors gave him some bad news. His condition would get no better. Through it all, Joseph was faithful, not only to being an usher, but also to playing our electronic *Scrabble* game when his pain would allow.

When the end of his life was near, the usher ministry gathered to celebrate what would be his final birthday on June 30th. Little did I know, earlier that morning, that I had played the last word I ever would with Joseph. Ironically, that last word was H-E-A-V-E-N. Not many days later, he died.

When I read the Resolution from our Church at his memorial service, I broke from normal protocol. Before this reading, I shared the friendship that Joseph and I had developed during his illness and how *Words with Friends* had kept us connected almost daily. I shared how God had entered our final game and that the last word played was HEAVEN.

I closed the remarks by saying, "I'll be ready to rematch him one day when he greets me as I too arrive in heaven." Before I could start reading, I was interrupted by applause.

Thoughts to ponder: What will you want people to remember about you when you're gone? What will your legacy be? Have you ever considered doing an audio or video about your life? Why not give it a try so people can know more than one side of you?

Chapter 4

Shared Stories

"There is no greater agony than bearing an untold story inside you."

Maya Angelou

This chapter consists of stories told to me by others, actual occurrences surrounding death and funerals. Each one has an element of humor that may turn a few tears into a smile or even laughter.

Quick Eulogy

The first two of the following stories were told by my pastor emeritus while we were in West Africa on a trip in 2010. He shared the true story of a gangster who had been killed. The family belonged to a church in Chicago, and they asked their pastor to have the funeral services there. The pastor stated that since the deceased was not a member of their congregation and was a notorious gangster, he didn't feel it would be feasible. After pleading with the pastor to make this exception, the family stated they would pay him well if he did. They would also make a sizable gift to the church on behalf of their loved one. The pastor said he would talk to his Board of Trustees and let them know the answer. After a meeting with his board, they concluded that since a substantial gift was to be made to the church, he should go ahead and acquiesce to the request. The pastor agreed and called the family to make arrangements for the services.

The day of the funeral arrived, and everything went well. The procession of the family, opening hymn, old and new testament scriptures, several tributes from the family, the reading of the obituary, and then a vocal solo all were completed in a timely fashion. Finally, it was time for the eulogy. The pastor stepped up to the pulpit, said a brief prayer, and then said, "Ladies and Gentlemen, Brothers and Sisters, here lies 'John Doe'. Everybody knows that John Doe was a bad man. But, last Friday night, John Doe met somebody who was 'badder' than he was. Undertakers, let's take him away." End of funeral. This must have been the quickest eulogy ever given.

Wrong Scripture

On that same trip to West Africa, when we got to Benin, our pastor emeritus, who was our West African Spiritual guide and tour leader, shared a true story from twenty years earlier.

One of our prominent members had passed away. His family wanted to have his service on the first Sunday of the month, which happened to be our busiest. With three services, baptism, communion, and Right Hand of Fellowship (reception of new members), the first Sundays are filled with activity. However, the family still chose to do this service at 3:00 in the afternoon on this first Sunday. The afternoon of the funeral arrived and the church was filled with those who had known the deceased and his family. The service got underway after the family had come in and were seated. The opening hymn was sung, and next was the reading of the sacred scriptures by two deacons. The Old

Testament was read without any problems. The New Testament scripture, read by the second deacon, had a different impact. The printed program stated that the scripture to be read was from 2 Corinthian 5:1, which reads:

> "For we know that if our earthly house of this tabernacle were dissolved, we have a building of God, a house not made with hands, eternal in the heavens." However, the deacon inadvertently read 1 Corinthians 5: 1, which has an entirely different context:

> "It is reported commonly that there is fornication among you, and such fornication as is not so much as named among the Gentiles, that one should have his father's wife."

"Well, if you could have only seen the looks on the faces of those assembled," stated our pastor emeritus. But the deacon's face didn't reveal he realized his mistake.

Note: Reading any material in public in advance is important to be sure it makes sense and is appropriate.

Soloist Found

A well-known funeral soloist at many funeral services in our area shared this story. A lady near death had told her daughter about a man she'd heard sing at a funeral and wanted him to sing at hers. Her mother had written down the soloist's name, but at the time of her passing, nobody knew who he was. The funeral home where her body was reposed contacted my friend and asked if he would do a solo, to which he agreed. The day of the services arrived and, when his part in the service came, he went to the microphone to bellow out the song he had selected; *"I won't complain."* After singing this popular song, the daughter stood to her feet and screamed out, "Mama, I tried to find the man you wanted to sing, and I didn't know whether we found him or not. But now I know we found the right man, and he sho nuff can sing!" My friend had been given an envelope with a check enclosed with a name close to his, but not exactly. However, when he took the $200 check to his bank they had no problem cashing it for him. They were used to seeing his name misspelled.

Goodbye Kiss

In another service where my friend was asked to sing, he reported another humorous experience he witnessed without needing to sing any notes. The daughter of the deceased came in to view her mother's body in the casket before the funeral got underway. The daughter was a heavy-set lady who was busty. My friend saw her walk up to the casket to view the body. After standing there for a few moments, she bent over to kiss her mother. When she tried to do this, her top-heaviness caused the casket to rock. Not giving up, she tried a second and a third time, with the same results. After the final try, she was heard saying, as she blew a kiss, "Goodbye, Mamma," and walked away.

Boat Rockin'

I had twice attempted to have a deacon-visit with a member who was hospitalized for about a month. She passed during that hospital stay. Due to another commitment on the Saturday of her funeral, I could not attend it, but my wife and I went to the visitation at the funeral home the evening before. As we entered the parlor where she lay at rest, we introduced ourselves to her husband and daughter. I had spoken with each on the phone during her hospitalization. They were a beautiful, distinguished-looking family. The deceased, who was in her late 60s, was elegantly adorned in her white coffin, which was surrounded with flowers. We stayed there for 30–45 minutes, mingling with family and guests.

That Sunday, while talking to one of my fellow deacons who had attended the services, he told me the major highlight of the funeral, which I had missed. Everything was going well, and the husband wanted to speak about his wife of more than twenty years. The husband began by thanking those in the congregation. He began to reflect upon the good marriage they'd had, reminiscing about the good times, especially the cruises they'd taken. Not only did he share about the cruises, but he described in detail the fact that most of the time on each cruise, they'd spent in their stateroom. He boasted they were 'rocking the boat' and 'tearing it up.' He even stated that once you get past 60, there's a little pill you can take that keeps your stamina going. They couldn't get enough of each other, and he would surely miss those romantic times.

My fellow deacon then said it got to the place it sounded as if he was advertising for his next cruising companion. The audience, as well as the clergy – our pastor and a catholic priest – were all laughing. When the priest got up to make his remarks, he looked at the husband and stated, "We are glad you enjoyed your life together, but I've never heard passion in a marriage described in such detail. I believe that might have been too much information for most of us."

Funeral Procession

My younger brother Lawrence, moved back to our hometown from New Jersey years ago, after our mother passed away. He told me the story of the VanMeter funeral. Our hometown has a population of about 35,000. He believed a large percentage of its residents had made it to the funeral of this prominent and large family. The funeral, he stated, took about two hours, and afterward, the funeral directors lined up the cars to head to the cemetery. It was one of those scorching summer days in Indiana. As far as the eye could see, hundreds of cars in the funeral procession headed to the deceased's final resting place in

Earlham Cemetery. Within a mile or so of the cemetery, the procession halted. People sat in their cars for a considerable length of time. What could possibly be the hold-up? I'm sure this was a question on everybody's mind, including my brother's. Finally, when the line got moving, and the entire procession had made it to the gravesite, the funeral director apologized to the assembled crowd. The reason for the long delay was that the fuel gauge on the hearse was not working, and the vehicle had run out of gas.

Comedian's Eulogy

If you had spent over three decades as a stand-up comedian in numerous venues throughout the country, how would you want to be remembered? My wife found out the answer to this question when she attended the funeral of funnyman 'Stan the Man.' Most funerals have a member of the clergy give the Words of Comfort – the eulogy – but when you are well known on the comedy circuit, why not have an even more renowned comedian do those honors? Well, that's just what happened at this life celebration. Had it not been for the fact that people were gathered in a church and there was a casket surrounded by flowers, one may have thought this was Comedy Night at the Apollo.

The service was jovial from start to finish. Not a dry eye in the place and that was not due to sorrow, but rather an atmosphere filled with comedy. Everyone on the program who gave remarks proved also to be a comedian, even if they were not. The eulogy given by an even more well-known national comedian seemed to think he was on a show stage instead of a church pulpit. He walked back and forth across the platform as he delivered one-liner after one-liner.

There are only 365 days in a year. What are the odds that a close friend or family member will die on your birthday? So it was with the comedian giving the Eulogy, or, might we say, the comedy routine?

This comedian shared with those in attendance that his best friend – the deceased – had sent him a birthday card with money in it for his birthday. He called his good friend the morning of his birthday to thank him and let him know that he and his wife had planned a romantic overnight stay at the Sybaris, a romantic getaway for married couples, for his birthday evening. That night, after getting to the lovers' resort, he was notified that his good friend, Stan the Man, had passed away. His wife had gone into the bathroom in their Sybaris suite to prepare for their romantic evening. Their suite had a pool, swing, and all the other romantic accouterments to make for an intimate evening between a man and his wife. But there he sat in the middle of the heart-shaped bed, naked. As his wife came from the bathroom in 'all her glory,' all he could do was sit there and cry over the news just received by text that his friend had died. "Why did his death have to take place on my birthday when we had this romantic evening planned?" No other commentary was made on the rest of the romantic evening. This national personality went on to share the highlights of his deceased friend's life and the years of comedy routines they had done together. Although the service was far more unorthodox than the average funeral, it was noted repeatedly by all those who had speaking parts that 'Stan the Man' would have wanted it this way. This Homegoing service was proof that funeral services do not have to be solemn occasions and that clergy members are not the only ones who can give the eulogy. I learned that even the funeral of comedian/actor Bernie Mac, had the same humorous Homegoing officiated by other comedians in the summer of 2008.

Thoughts to ponder: Do you want a Homegoing/funeral service? If yes, do you want it to be a solemn occasion in your remembrance or a joyful celebration of your life? Will you request a particular type/color of clothing be worn, or other particulars be included?

Chapter 5

Unfamiliar Funerals

"Grief is the price we pay for love."

Colin Murray Parkes

African Funerals

I retired from the financial planning field June 30, 2010, a highlight, to be sure. But an even bigger highlight was our trip to West Africa, 15 days later in July. My wife and I loved traveling, and Africa was one of the trips on our list. The trip, led by our pastor emeritus, had a total of twelve journeyers who would travel to Ghana, Togo, and Benin. I remember the orientation we went through months before our journey. One of the major items covered included immunization. There were shots and pills necessary to prevent us from contracting diseases that could prove fatal. We learned there were 16 different illnesses that we could be subject to, the main one, malaria. We also ascertained that the water, food, and insects were the three major things that would cause us much harm if we were not careful. I said to my wife, "Remind me why we want to go to Africa since our travels there could be fatal?"

After months of preparing for this big adventure, the time for our flight to Accra, Ghana, had come. The flight time was about 14 hours. I remember our flight leaving Chicago's O'Hare Airport that took us first to Washington, D.C., then to Accra. I had heard fellow African Americans who had been to Africa claim that getting to Africa was like coming home. I had often thought, how can this be for someone who has never been to Africa? Well, after arriving at the Accra Airport, it didn't take long to understand that although my wife and I had never been there, our spirits recognized our ancestral land. We now also knew the feeling, so many of our African American brothers and sisters felt after their first visit to the motherland.

Our tour soon was off and going. The first day we started after a thirty-minute oration by our pastor emeritus. Our first full day there in Accra was a Saturday. On our itinerary was a visit to a shop where coffins were made. I thought to myself, could that really be something of interest for us to see? Once we arrived at this facility, how shocked we first-timers were. The coffins most Ghanaians used were custom-made by craftsmen who built a coffin based on how the person had lived or died. For example, had the deceased been a fisherman, the coffin was made to resemble a big fish. Had the person been a teacher, it was like a big book. A carpenter's coffin resembled a hammer. If the deceased had worked for the airline industry, the final resting bed looked like an airplane. In addition to occupational-type coffins, some coffins communicated the cause of death. There were actual coffins that looked like a pack of cigarettes for those who had smoked and died from lung cancer; liquor bottles for some who drank themselves to death … and the list went on and on.

We learned that the people of Ghana revere the dead so much that funerals are a part of their social life. When we in America speak of celebrating a life, our rituals are nowhere as elaborate as in Ghana. Most funerals are held on weekends. Families with money advertise the funeral, often with billboards. Some families spend as much on funerals as on weddings, if not more.

Since our first day of touring was a Saturday, it was not long after we visited the 'coffin factory' that we encountered several funerals in various parts of the city. Each of the celebrations we witnessed from our tour bus was filled with people in the streets. The mourners were all dressed in red and black – traditional funeral clothing in Ghana. In addition to the festivities, the bereaved families provided food, drinks, and music. For outsiders, it resembled a party, unlike the solemn funerals we had experienced in most places in the United States. Funeral rites also involve people who come to mourn and to shed tears. In ancient times, professional mourners were paid by the volumes of tears they cried. They carried little chalices beneath their eyes to catch the tears as they marched in the funeral parade. While some parts of the services are like American funerals, they are far more festive.

Religious Practices

The only funerals I have witnessed outside of the United States have been in Ghana. I learned that other countries worldwide, have similar festive practices. In Indonesia, funerals usually involve the entire village and can last for days or even a week or more. In Australia, the aborigines have a ritual that starts with a smoking ceremony in the loved one's living area to help drive away their spirit. The body is placed atop a type of platform and then covered in leaves and left to decompose. After this ritual, the mourners start the celebration with food and dance. In Mongolia and Tibet, Buddhists believe in the transmigration of spirits, the movement of a soul into another body after death or more commonly referred to as reincarnation. They chop up the body into many pieces and place it on a mountain top to be exposed to the elements. In the Philippines, there are also some unique practices, one of which involves blindfolding the deceased and dressing them in their best clothes.

Death in other world religions involves their own rituals that vary. Formal mourning in Jewish tradition is divided into four periods, from the death and burial to the unveiling of the tombstone with the person's Hebrew name, at the end of the first year following death. In Islam, the person is always buried as soon after death as possible, and the body is ritually cleansed before the burial. In Hinduism, the rituals extend for 12 days. They believe in reincarnation, and the purpose of mourning death is to help the deceased achieve the best possible rebirth, rather than finding everlasting peace. On the funeral day, the body is anointed and decorated with flowers and led by a procession to be cremated.

I have discovered that religions worldwide have many traditions and customs surrounding death. Most faiths follow procedures when it comes to memorial services without the body or using the urn with the remains left for the service. Many funeral services with the body present will later cremate, bury or entomb the remains much as we do in the United States.

Regardless of where people live in this world, they will die. How survivors deal with the celebration of life varies from country to country, but it is something we all must face. I have found that those with a religious foundation often tend to feel that life does not end at death. Does it mean that those who believe in God or a supreme being grieve and mourn less? Not necessarily.

Death is still a great mystery, regardless of our faith and beliefs. Grief counseling, one form of therapy, aims to help those who experience emotional, physical, and spiritual reactions deal with their loss, and is available in many parts of the world. Support groups in many places let those grieving and mourning know they do not have to go through the process alone.

Other Beliefs

Death doesn't take a holiday. My wife and I had made plans for her birthday celebration one year when we were notified of the death of a friend of about ten years. Our friend's wake was on my wife's birthday, with the funeral the following day. This family was of different faith, and we had never been to a funeral of someone of their religion. It didn't matter to me because we had been friends with this family and had often been invited to fellowship with them on other occasions.

My wife's birthday arrived and, as the evening approached, I mentioned that we needed to get dressed to go to the visitation at the funeral home some twenty to thirty minutes away. Her response was, "It's my birthday, and we have plans." I responded, "I'm fully aware of the plans we have for this evening, but stopping by the visitation to offer our condolences to this family who lost its matriarch will not interfere with your birthday plans. By doing the visitation, we will have the chance to speak with family members and extend our condolences. That may not happen if we only go to the funeral tomorrow." Because it was her birthday and we already had plans, going to the funeral the next day was what she preferred.

Not to belabor the point or spoil our evening plans for her birthday, I told her I would go to the visitation and come back home, then we could proceed with our evening plans. To that suggestion, I got the silent treatment. Two things I have found we husbands have difficulty dealing with are the silent treatment and tears. After getting dressed, I left for the visitation. I viewed the body and offered my family's condolences to the husband, his four children, and several grandchildren. I completed all of this, and from the time I left home until the time I returned, only 90 minutes had passed. My wife got over being mad with me, I guess, and we went on to enjoy the rest of her birthday evening.

The next day was the funeral. We were among the first to arrive for the service in their temple. We had never set foot in one of these ornate structures before and were unfamiliar with their customs, especially for funerals. Upon arrival, we found our way in and took a seat with the few who also had arrived early. The service was about to start – the closed casket carrying the deceased was led in by the clergy, followed by the family. My wife and I tried to fit in, but it was apparent we were outsiders. The prayers, songs, readings and eulogy were all in their native language, which we did not speak. The service was quite lengthy and, after almost three hours, I leaned over and whispered in my wife's ear, "Don't you wish you had gone with me to the visitation last night instead?" She gave me a sheepish smile as we continued to experience a service honoring the life of our recently departed friend.

The most important thing is that grief transcends all people and faiths. The ministry of presence, showing the family you took time to come and be with them during their time of bereavement, is what matters most.

Pet Funerals

Of the many hundreds of funerals I have attended, the only one I have not experienced and is not as common, is one for a pet. For many pet owners, their pet is as much a member of their family as any human. When a pet dies, whether it is a dog, cat, bird, or any other type of creature, the family still goes through a period of grief.

A good friend with whom I was traveling to an out-of-town football game shared with me the story of a woman whose dog had died from cancer. I have learned that animals often experience the same diseases as humans. The lady had sought out the services of a pet funeral home. The day she went to view the remains of her beloved pet, she suffered a massive heart attack and died. Her family decided to have both the woman's funeral and that of her beloved canine at the same time.

My friend and his wife both attended the funeral at an area funeral home. The lady was in her casket while her beloved pet was laid in a pet casket right next to it. He told me his wife also sang at the funeral, which was like most funerals, except that many people also brought their pets. Comforting words were spoken, not only about the lady but also about her pet. Both were later to be cremated. There was a repast with a wide assortment of foods for the guests. As everyone began to get their plates, the guests were asked to wait until the pets had been served first. Yes, there was food for the four-legged guests as well, and they too needed to be served.

Over the years, I have had a few pets. I understand how attached one can become to them. When a pet dies, there is that sense of loss, and family members usually go through a period of mourning. It's to be understood that it's normal. Vetstreet – www.vetstreet.com – a service that delivers advice from veterinarians for families grieving the loss of a pet, offers the following strategies for coping when you lose a pet:

1. **Talk it through**. Find people you can talk to about your pet.

2. **Address any feelings of guilt**. A pet may have been euthanized, and the pet owner struggles with the guilt of having had to make the choice to put their beloved pet down. Don't think of it as taking your pet's life but see it as a privilege and a gift to spare them the pain and suffering when there was nothing that could have been done to keep them alive any longer.

3. **Consider a Ceremony**. These pet ceremonies can be an occasion to gather friends and family to say goodbye and celebrate the pet's life.

4. **If you have children, help them with remembrances**. Children feel the loss much more intensely than adults. For many, it's their first experience with death. Encourage them to talk about their sadness and give them time to work through their pain.

5. **Take your time**. Grief is an individual process. Deal with your grief as long as you need to and don't feel rushed to get over your sorrow.

6. **Tie up loose ends.** If you have lingering questions or doubts about how your pet died, see your veterinarian to get your questions answered.

7. **Memorialize your pet.** Find a way that is meaningful to you to honor your pet. Planting trees, making a donation to a favorite animal charity, or having your pet's remains placed in a memorial urn are among the options available to keep your pet's memory alive.

Children Funerals

I have only attended a few funeral services for children. These little ones who have yet to lead what we may call a whole life are among the saddest occasions I have experienced.

The first infant funeral I attended some years ago was for a child less than one year old. Walking into this church and viewing the infant casket, seemed so unfair. The child barely had a chance to know anything about the world or live its life. The child's casket was surrounded by floral arrangements, toys, and teddy bears. I remember looking down at that beautiful baby in his tiny casket, greeting the family, and taking my seat. What can you say that might make a difference to a grieving couple who are in the midst of burying their infant son? I probably uttered words to the effect of "My condolences on your loss," – words that may have been shared a number of times already – words entirely inadequate to let the family know how much you care about them. Those parents may or may not remember what you said that day, or even your presence, but after it's all over, you were one of many who helped them through this acute time of mourning.

One of our church members, Becky, shared with me that one of her most difficult experiences was the death of her grandson who passed away under the age of one. She told me how much support the church gave her during this painful time. She gave me a poem titled

To All Parents. She told me she still reads it often. Although the poem was written for parents who have lost a child, she said the loss of a grandchild is doubly difficult. Grandparents grieve their son's or daughter's loss, as well as the loss of their grandchild. Becky, also let me know their family decided against having the six-month-old placed in an infant casket and chose a baby crib instead for the Homegoing, having the child's body surrounded by stuffed animals and other playthings. They felt it would lessen the pain by having it appear the child went to sleep at night and woke up in heaven the following day. Also, they chose burial in the children's section of the cemetery.

Becky cited two other resources that helped her family through this time. One was the Service of Remembrance our church has every December for those who have lost a loved one during that year or before. She gave me a copy also of a short poem titled *Christmas in Heaven* she received during the service:

I see the countless trees around the world below,
with tiny lights like heaven's stars, reflecting on the snow.
the sight is so spectacular; please wipe away that tear,
for I am spending Christmas with Jesus Christ this year.
I hear the many Christmas songs that people hold so dear,
but the sounds of music can't compare with the Christmas choir up here.
I have no words to tell you, the joy words do bring
for it is beyond description the songs the angels sing.
I know how much you miss me,
I see the pain inside your heart,
but I am not so far away, we really aren't apart.
So be happy for me, my dear ones. You know I hold you dear,
and be glad I'm spending Christmas with Jesus Christ this year.
I send you each a special gift from my heavenly home above
I send you each a memory of my undying love.
After all, love is the gift, more precious than pure gold,
it was always most important in the stories Jesus told.
Please love and keep each other, as my Father said to do,
for I can't count the blessings or love that He has for you.

So have a Merry Christmas and wipe away that tear.
Remember that I'm spending Christmas with Jesus Christ this year.

The second resource she told me about turned out to be of great support for her family. They were Compassionate Friends – www.compassionatefriends.org – an organization founded in 1969 as a peer support group for parents who have lost a child. The group exists to provide friendship, understanding, and hope to those going through the natural grieving process.

The youngest funeral I attended was for a newborn who lived only minutes. The mother gave an eloquent summation of the nine months of carrying her daughter, all the way until her c-section delivery and holding her newborn until the child turned blue. The minister had prepared Words of Comfort for the family, but once the mother finished, all that was left was for him to give the benediction. Upon exiting the funeral parlor, the family gave out an inscribed button with the newborn's name and one date 02/14/2020 on it, along with a bookmark that read;

An angel in the book of life
Wrote down Kulture's birth,
Then whispered as she closed the book…
Too beautiful for earth.
February 14, 2020
8:07am, 6lbs 1 oz.

If there is a lighter side to children dying, it could only be they are spared the pain and suffering so many people go through in this life. Yet, we think about who they might have become. Our focus now should be on the precious time when we had them with us and the chance, we will have to spend with them in eternity someday. That truly can give us blessed hope.

Quarantined Tears

The start of a new decade arrived with the year 2020. We already had a lot of plans in place for the year ahead; numerous parties, vacation travel to the nation's capital, a family reunion in Texas, and many more weekly activities. Early in the first quarter of the year, life as we had known was about to change. News stories began to be broadcast about a virus spreading in Asia.

My first thought was that that's many miles away, and it does not impact the western world. It didn't take long before the name *Coronavirus* (COVID-19) extended beyond Asia. In a matter of weeks, the World Health Organization declared a pandemic. This virus had finally made its entrance into the United States. It had already proven deadly in Asia and Europe. Daily newscasts announced the number of cases confirmed state by state. As news spread, the panicked public began to empty store shelves of needed supplies. The first commodities to become unavailable were toilet tissue and hand sanitizer. Next, celebrities who had been diagnosed with COVID-19 made the news. Sporting events, the theater, and other activities were canceled from state to state.

Like everyone else, I watched the chain of events due to COVID-19. I continued my daily activities and followed the protocols recommended by the Centers for Disease Control. *How long will this last?* I wondered. The reality hit when some states, including my own, Illinois, put in place a stay-at-home mandate. Schools, stores, businesses, and what seemed like the whole world was on lock down. Of one thing I felt sure – funerals would continue.

The week that our Illinois Governor Pritzker ordered the stay-at-home mandate, I had funerals on my calendar for Tuesday and Thursday. The Tuesday funeral was for the mother of a couple I knew from our Married Couples Ministry. She was born in 1919, the same year as my mother. It was on St. Patrick's Day, but her family had her arrayed in her favorite color, red, not green. Red roses surrounded her casket. We had a crowd that had already begun to practice 'social distancing,' a new phrase made ubiquitous by this pandemic. I spoke with the family during the visitation period, and my part of the service was reading the New Testament scripture. After leaving the Homegoing service, I stopped to pick up a few items from the crowded store and hurried home, where I'd stay until the following funeral.

Thursday arrived, and I was up, preparing to attend the second Homegoing of that week. That morning, I was at my desk when my wife came downstairs and into my office. "Did you read the email from our church?" she asked. I had just given it a cursory overview and moved on. She told me that new protocols were in place, giving our congregation direction during this time of calamity.

Sunday worship services would now be streamed live for our 7:30 a.m., 11:00 a.m., and 6:00 p.m. services. Our midweek services would also be streamed live. Our member and guest services teams and other ministry partners would make wellness checks each Thursday to our seniors and other vulnerable members of our community. Technology was now the emphasis for Facebook Live with the pastor, his podcasts, weekly devotionals, and robocalls to keep our members abreast of church news and more. The reality hit me when I read the new funeral guidelines, which would be in place till further notice. The statement read:

When a person in our community passes, **ONLY** *the immediate family will be the primary concern for the funeral services. The funeral will be live-streamed and recorded for extended family and friends of the deceased. We will practice social distancing for all Homegoing services. Family members and everyone else participating in the service must be at least six feet away from each other. All deacons and ushers must wear masks and gloves when participating in the service.*

What got my attention was the following line, in bold, which read:

No seniors (65 years old and older), or any person with a compromised immune system, should participate in a Homegoing service at Trinity United Church of Christ or at other churches or funeral homes.

My wife reminded me that I was in that demographic and needed to stay home. I told her, "I know I'm over 65, but I'm in reasonably good health. And as long as I follow the precautions, like washing my hands, wearing gloves, and maybe even a mask, I should be okay." She looked me in the eye and declared, "You will keep your butt at home. I will go to that funeral in your place." From the look on her face and her tone of voice, I knew she meant business. I stayed home.

The hard reality for me was that I am truly a senior citizen, even though I still feel young at heart. But my age – just a number, right? – had suddenly caught up with me.

For the first time, there was a 'new normal' for funerals, not experienced in my lifetime. I streamed the Homegoing services at noon and saw the small number of family members seated, six feet apart, on every other pew. No hugging, no handshakes. A sense of sadness permeated the sanctuary I had never seen at Homegoing services. From that moment, I could see that funerals for the foreseeable future had changed. This is what I was feeling, watching from home a service I had planned to attend. As one of the family members who gave a tribute for her departed loved one stated, "This seems so surreal." I could relate.

Staying at home the second Sunday in a row, streaming our church service, we also watched *CBS News Sunday Morning*. This episode focused on the pandemic we were experiencing. The statement that caught my attention near the end of the 90-minute-long program further put the pandemic in perspective. After the host gave a litany of life events impacted by it, he stated, "Loved ones can't come together in great numbers to mourn, as funerals have changed. How do you quarantine tears?"

How much longer will this new paradigm remain in place? Will the world ever be the same after COVID-19? I believe in my heart that this virus just may be the thing to bring people together like never before. As the *Sunday Morning* commentator suggested in his closing thought, "Love really does conquer all. We just may be getting a new start."

I nodded my head in agreement, feeling, Yes, we are **all** in this together.

Thoughts to ponder: What do you dislike about going to funerals? Think back to a funeral(s) that was inspirational to you. What was it about those services that you remember the most? What will you need to do in the event of a future pandemic?

Chapter 6

Spoken Words

"Be yourself. Everyone else is already taken."

Oscar Wilde

A statement was made at a funeral I attended years ago in Kansas City that made me think about how people react to those who are different from them. During this service for a young man who had died from AIDS, the minister stated, "There are two things Christians have difficulty understanding: death and human sexuality."

For many years, homosexuality has been a controversial subject in many circles, including the church. The question quite often has been whether a person is born this way or is it a learned or chosen behavior and lifestyle? I do not have the answer, but I know that with the legalization of same-sex marriage, the question will not go away. At this funeral in Kansas City, it was the only statement made that those at the service were left to ponder.

The first service I recall participating in for a same-gender-loving man I had known many years was held at our church.. The service was very dignified, and his life partner was visibly in mourning. The associate minister who gave the Words of Comfort did not try to hide the sexuality of the deceased. She tastefully orated about the many good qualities in this brother's life, but most importantly, the relationship he had with the Lord.

Son's Confession

A couple of years later, I was assigned to have a deacon visit with a parishioner who had been placed in hospice care. After entering the living room of his home, his wife introduced me to her husband, who was wasting away from cancer. He lay there in his hospital bed, in and out of consciousness. I spent more time chatting with his wife and being there as a ministry of presence to comfort her during her husband's final days. For the next few weeks, I would call and check in with her to pray and offer any other assistance on behalf of the church. Finally, when his death came, she called the church as well as me and two other deacons who had visited during her husband's time in home hospice.

The day for his Homegoing service arrived, and I was there to greet his widow and other family members during the visitation and pre-past, being a continental breakfast. The service went well, and, as in most services I have attended, the tributes, the reading of the obituary, and the Words of Comfort gave me a better picture of the life of the deceased. After the eulogy, the funeral directors were called forward to remove the floral arrangements and casket from the sanctuary so the procession to the cemetery could begin. While all this preparation was taking place, a young man in what appeared to be in his mid-to-late 30s hastily made his way to the pulpit to talk to the presiding minister. After a brief conversation, the minister stopped the proceedings to introduce the young man.

The deceased had been married twice before, and the widow was his third wife. The minister asked the congregation to stay where they were as he introduced the son of the deceased from his first marriage, letting everyone know the young man had something to say. The son was given the microphone as all eyes were on him.

The son spoke of the distant relationship he and his father had during his growing up and even into adulthood. His father had rejected him because he was gay, but had tried to keep it hidden. He explained his father had disapproved of his lifestyle. The two of them always argued during their limited times together in his adult years. By now, tears streamed down his face as he described the pain he felt all these years because his father did not accept him for who he was. The son's confession went on for 15–20 minutes.

After he finished, the minister embraced him and asked the congregation to lift their hands toward him as he prayed for him. After the prayer, the son walked beside the minister behind his father's casket. At the entrance to the sanctuary, they paused to greet those who were exiting. One by one, I watched as person after person embraced the son, demonstrating an outpouring of love and support to a young man whose father had not shown it. I overheard him tell the minister as everyone was preparing to depart for the cemetery that he was not a member of any church. But because of the outpouring of love and acceptance that day, when the time came for him to make up his mind about becoming a Christian, this was the church where he could certainly find love and not condemnation.

I'm not sure if I have seen the son since his father's funeral. But I'm sure the acceptance he felt that day left a lasting impression that spoke volumes to him. The acceptance paved the way to help with the grief and, in due time, his decision to discipleship. The outpouring of acceptance by those in attendance showed compassion that I have never seen exhibited. If others felt like I did, they probably had a sense of being a part of this young man's healing. His coming forth at the end of his father's funeral helped provide the closure needed for this young man to move on with his life, knowing a burden was lifted from his shoulders.

Match Making

A friend named Robert was one of the people God used to start my involvement in prison ministry. Sherri and I had met him at a wedding reception over ten years before. Robert worked for an organization that helped ex-offenders – 'returning citizens,' as we prefer to call them – return to society after their release from prison. Robert and I maintained contact from that time forward. A few times he had invited us to programs at the Methodist Church of which he was an active member and lay-leader. I got to know him much better and found him to be a wealth of knowledge about many of life's issues, including the prison system. When Robert's health began to decline around 2016, he occasionally called me needing help getting to his doctor's appointments, to the store, and other places after he was unable to drive.

On Independence Day, my wife and I invited him and a senior lady from our church named Eva for a picnic at our home. Sherri and I thought they might be a good match to comfort each other with their senior health ailments. As I recall, we had BBQ, potato salad, hot dogs, hamburgers, baked beans, salad, and dessert. After dinner, I went to my home office to get him a saved obituary program from the funeral of a mutual friend who had passed the previous month. He had been unable to attend that funeral and asked me to save him a copy. After reading through this program, which was quite elaborate and costly, he stated, "When my time comes, my family would never go to the expense of such a service for me." My wife and I responded, "We know your church will be there for you. After all, you've been a lay leader for many years. Your church is your spiritual family. Certainly, they will step up to honor your life and legacy."

During our holiday meal, I encouraged Robert and Eva to get to know each other better. I thought a spark just might have been ignited during their time together. It was only after I had driven Eva to her apartment that evening that Robert dropped a bombshell on me. After she was in her apartment and I started to drive him to his condo, he said, "Eva is a nice lady, but I must let you know I have no interest in her … because I'm gay. My family has known this for years and not accepted me for it, but I have never let anyone in the church know about my sexual orientation for fear of being further rejected." I'm glad we were stopped at a traffic light because I never expected to hear those words spoken – not from Robert. There may have been a mishap had I been moving in traffic. Just seven weeks later, he was to make his transition from earth to eternity.

Robert's memorial service at his Methodist Church was well attended. The individuals on the program gave great tributes. However, the dinner after the service in a hotel banquet room – hosted by his family – was quite elaborate. I believe that in his later years, his family had become reconciled to who he was and provided a fitting memorial to celebrate his love, life, and legacy.

Grief Denial

Many times throughout our lives, we may experience periods of grief. Although we think of death as the ultimate cause of grief, other situations can also bring it about. The ending of a relationship, financial or job loss, or diagnosis of a terminal illness can be just as devastating. When any of these has occurred, many experience denial. Reactions may include fear, shock, avoidance, confusion, and more. At this stage, many feel life makes no sense, has no meaning, and is so overwhelming that one refuses to deal with the issues at hand. It may take days, weeks, or months for the denial to start to fade and the healing process to begin.

Men are often in denial more than women. We men are told to 'man up.' We hear, "Men don't cry," and therefore, we keep it all on the inside. One man I know named Tom, who lost both his wife and two children in a tragic auto accident, appeared to be coping with everything well during the week of preparation for the services and through the end of that period. However, Tom refused to go to any grief support group or get counseling.

Within a matter of weeks, his grief, denial, and mourning had taken him to the pits of despair. Drugs and alcohol became his coping mechanism and, some eight years later, he had still not recovered. After losing family, job, home, and everything else that was once important to him, he found himself going from shelter to shelter.

After a prolonged period, he finally came to the end of his rope. Tom entered an alcohol and drug rehabilitation program and, after a number of months, was set free from these substances that had so dramatically changed his life. All because he refused to deal with his grief and mourning, he suffered many years that may have been avoided. Today, he's back, living an everyday life and realizing he has much for which to live.

Most of us have come to realize that not every person is fully capable of seeing their way through the pain and suffering of grief. People need a way to share their story, express their grief, and be heard.

However, when grief comes – in whatever form – get help. An abundance of support is available. You do not have to go through it by yourself.

Thoughts to Ponder: Is there anything you wish to remain private and take to your grave? What would you want somebody to say about you at your funeral? Write it down and let your family know.

Chapter 7

Life Celebrations

I have fought a good fight, I have finished my course, I have kept the faith; Henceforth there is laid up for me a crown of righteousness, which the Lord, the righteous judge shall give me at that day; and not me only, but unto all them also that love his appearing.

2 Timothy 4: 8–9 KJV

I have been to many services that were truly life celebrations. Many such services stand out in my mind, which left me feeling honored that the person whose life we were celebrating had been an inspiration to many, including me. Here are just a few that had a significant impact on my life:

Minister's Farewell

The Homegoing Celebration for our Minister for the Sick and Shut-in significantly impacted me. She had served in that capacity at Trinity United Church of Christ for many years, and only needed to complete her studies to be ordained. She had been a nurse, and compassion was innate for her. She was in and out of hospitals, nursing homes, and residences ministering to the sick and shut-in six days a week. You knew when she was at church because her car was in the parking lot with a bike rack and bike on the trunk. If her calls took her to any of the hospitals or other rehab facilities in downtown Chicago, weather permitting, she would park her car at one facility and bike to the others. Not only did that give her exercise, but it also was more economical ... parking downtown is expensive.

Although she had served in this capacity for some time, she also completed her Master of Divinity degree to be ordained in the United Church of Christ. When the time came to go before our Ecclesiastical Council, she was ready because she'd already been ministering in this area and was well known throughout the Chicago Metropolitan Association for her work. Her Ecclesiastical Council hearing was well attended and left nobody any doubt that she was well prepared for the area of ministry to which she had been called.

When her ordination date was set for December, I was honored to be one of three asked to read scripture at the service. She had sent all three of us a group text message asking us to participate. She stated first that the reason for asking was because of our Christian commitment to ministry. Secondly, she chose us because we were good orators (she didn't want us to be too high-minded). There were ten deacons whom she'd kept abreast of her visitations with members of our congregation at hospitals and other medical facilities. She often sent text messages and, on many occasions, she'd ask one of us ten to assist if she had been unable to see someone who needed a visit. Only two months after her ordination, she sent a text that left me dismayed. I imagine the other nine on the text were equally alarmed.

It was February 8th that we received what would be the last text message from her. It read: "My Deacon team, Hey, I got some rough news. Part 1 – Tuesday. I spent Monday night in the hospital for pain in my side for the last two to three weeks. It turns out to be metastatic cancer of the breast and liver, a profound case. I am meeting with a doctor tomorrow to discuss comfort measures. I don't plan to fight the obvious. We all have to die once. I am taking this as my once with palliative care. Part 2 – today Wednesday. I'm just getting home, been gone since 9:00 a.m., exhausted. All was good at the palliative care meeting, the nurse practitioner was excellent. My daughter was with me while my son, who is out of state, listened in on the phone. The nurse practitioner insists I get a more definitive diagnosis, like the type of cancer. They want a biopsy and more tests. The practitioner has connected me with an oncologist. I will meet with him tomorrow. I am too tired to talk, I have canceled my trip to Mexico, scheduled for Friday, and I go to Heaven instead, lol – have to keep our humor. I talked to the pastors last night. It's not a secret. I just wanted my pastoral staff and deacon ministry to know first, before Facebook. Don't call me, text only. Be safe. You are doing a great job caring for the congregation. Feel free to share with other deacons. It's prayer time church – LOL. No calls, too many, too exhausting."

I sent her a text message and flowers shortly afterwards. On April 15th, I was busy helping my wife prepare our home for guests. She was having a dozen of her lady friends over late that afternoon, and we were also awaiting a youth group from Germany who would be in the Chicago area for a week. My wife and I were the host family for a married couple who were chaperones for the group.

Around 2:00, I was at a stopping point in helping my wife get prepared, but instead of heading to the church to pick up our guests from Germany, I felt an urge first to see our Minister of the Sick and Shut-in, who was in her final days of hospice care. I headed to her hospital room, where family and friends had gathered. I greeted everyone as I entered the room and went to talk with her daughter, who was seated at her bedside. The hospice nurses had told her that her mother could hear what was being said but could not respond.

I spoke softly to her and read a couple of passages of scripture. Her daughter then asked everyone to circle her mother's bed while I led them in prayer. As I left the hospital, my cell phone rang. One of our ministers let me know the couple from Germany was waiting for me to pick them up. I arrived a few minutes before 4:30 and greeted the couple, apologizing for my tardiness, and explaining why it had taken me longer to get there. We loaded their luggage into my car and proceeded home, where the ladies had been gathered since around 4 o'clock. The husband from Germany joined me on my deck while his wife joined the women inside our home. In a few hours, I got the word that our Minister for the Sick and Shut-in had "answered God's call and returned home to that beautiful City of Zion," as her obituary later would read. It was at that point, when I was glad, I had not put my visit with her off until Monday. It would have been too late.

The Homegoing service took place the following Friday. It was only the fifth time in my twenty-three years at my church that I had seen the balcony, as well as the main sanctuary, filled to capacity for a funeral service. As the service got underway, the family was escorted in, led by the bike she had used in her visits to facilities in the downtown area. The pulpit was filled with ministers, and the choir was filled with members of our many choirs. My wife and I were there, along with our guest couple from Germany. The celebration flowed with each scripture read, each prayer spoken, each song sung, each tribute given, and, finally, the Words of Comfort from our senior pastor, all ministered to those in attendance. The finale, however, that brought everyone to tears was the benediction given by her son, while the Dance Ministry performed to the song titled *Total Praise*. Her son's powerful and spirit-filled words spoken in the benediction for his mother gave us to know that soon there would be another minister in the immediate family. In my sanctified imagination, I could see his mother dancing in heaven as that benediction was given.

Distinguished Service

Two and a half years later, we celebrated the life of one of our elder deacons. He and his wife, also an ordained deacon, had been married for twenty-four years and were participants in our Married Couples Ministry. We often referred to them as our 'Icons of Love.' If you came into his presence during the 24 years they were married, you would hear him joyously declare (in his professed not-so-good English), "I AIN'T never had it so good!" This described his marriage to his beloved wife, always by his side. His life of almost 87 years had been a blessing to so many. In the years I had known him, he was an encouragement to men younger than he and, along with his wife, had helped to save several marriages. His tall demeanor and soft-spoken voice would get your attention, and your focus would be on his words of wisdom.

After a lengthy illness, he was placed in hospice. His wife invited some friends, deacons, and ministers to their home to celebrate what would be his final communion service. As the invitation stated, it was not to say Goodbye, but rather to say Hello.

During his Homegoing service, I got a better sense of the military. Although he hadn't served in any branch of the United States Military, at his memorial service our pastor emeritus elevated him to the rank of 5-Star General in the Army of the Lord. During those Words of Comfort, our pastor emeritus eloquently elaborated what each star represented in the life of our Elder Deacon. Each one began with the letter **L**.

The first star symbolized his **Love for Life**. He had lived his life to the fullest, and anyone who knew him understood that love.

The second star was for **Learning**. He was a man who enjoyed learning so that he could share that learning with others who crossed his path in and outside of the church.

The third L star stood for **Laborers.** He was always working for the Lord and was an integral part in inspiring others to be laborers for the Lord as well.

The fourth star was for his **Lady**, the love of his life, his wife, who had made his last 24 years even more meaningful.

The final L in the five stars symbolized his **Love for the Lord**. His reason for living was to serve the Lord, and that he did.

Therefore, as it was summed up, we could all salute this high-ranking soldier for a job well done in the Army of the Lord.

Posthumous Recognition

Another life celebration I will long remember took place on my birthday some years ago, before I retired and began serving as a deacon. This brother had been our Minister of Music for many years. On the day of his Homegoing service, his body lay in state in our sanctuary from Noon until 7:00, the time of his funeral. Again, this service was well attended, and a splendid musical tribute was performed to honor his musical genius. In addition to all the tributes and other parts of the service, a special service bestowed upon him a Doctorate of Music, posthumously. That was the first time I had seen such honor conferred. The service lasted four hours. I was there for at least five. The most memorable part was when I got home, close to midnight. My wife said, "I thought you went to a funeral," and then added, "Did you go somewhere else after the service?" I responded, "No, it was just a lengthy celebration of life for a great man."

It's only during celebrations like these I have described that you feel honored to have known individuals who impacted the lives of so many.

Active Senior

There have been many people who have touched my life whom I will never forget. A former colleague fits this description. I socialized with people I worked with, while others remained at-work acquaintances only.

I will call her Daisy, to begin with, and you will see why a bit later. Daisy was in the accounting field before working at this national financial planning firm in 1983. Not many people pursue a new career field at 59 years of age, but Daisy did. I first met her in 1992 while working in our corporate office in Kansas City. After I relocated to Chicago in 1996 to become a manager at one of our six Chicagoland offices, I saw her a bit more frequently at area meetings held for our six Chicagoland offices. She had a proven track record and was one of our top producers for several years. Not only did she do financial planning, but she still prepared over 250 tax returns a year for private clients. One thing I found interesting about Daisy was how youthful she was, now in her 70s. When the weather was nice, and she had appointments close to her own community, she often put on her rollerblades to head to those meetings. She did this until almost age 80 when her family let her know, it was time to get off the rollerblades and drive the car with four wheels. I really got to know Daisy after I retired in 2010.

The following year, another colleague – another trailblazer in our industry – lost her husband. Shortly after that, a number of us got together with her to provide support. She wanted her associates to be involved in fellowship, and her choice was a monthly game called Michigan Rummy. About a year into the monthly card games, Daisy, who had preceded me in retirement by several years, was now at a stage where driving was a challenge outside of her small community. Since we would rotate monthly among a number of different homes, I agreed to pick her up and bring her so she too had the chance to keep abreast of what was going on in the company, as I was doing. It was always a delight because each month she had a good joke to tell me. I've shared many jokes that I learned from Daisy. During those times, we also talked about current events, politics (although we did not usually agree), the company we both had been a part of, and our faith. Over the next seven years, we became the best of friends.

In 2017 she had a fall and spent a couple of months in rehab. I drove to Indiana, where she was doing her rehab, and finally got to meet her son, about whom she had told me so much. Not too long after that visit to her rehab facility, I was again picking her up to play Michigan Rummy. We played the game using dimes and not dollars. During our sessions, any of us playing would win or lose a dollar to as much as $5.00. We were not meeting for the gambling, but rather socializing.

In the latter part of 2017, her health changed, and she passed away in January of 2018. When my wife and I went to the visitation, her family immediately recognized me, although I had only met her son. They all knew it was me who drove Miss Daisy to the monthly games, but she sat in the front seat. I was her friend, not her chauffeur (as Morgan Freeman and Jessica Tandy acted in the 1989 movie *Driving Miss Daisy*).

The day of her services at a funeral home on Chicago's southwest side was attended by less than 200 people. But those of us who were there knew the many lives she touched, and we shared those stories. Although the officiating minister did not know her, his Words of Comfort seemed as if her best friend had given them. My wife and I accompanied the family to the cemetery less than three miles from our home. We still have our monthly games. Although Daisy is no longer at the table, her name comes up often just the same, as our memory of her lingers on.

Thoughts to ponder: Whose life have you touched, who will treasure the lessons you have taught them by being who you are? What have you done to keep the memory of a loved one alive?

Chapter 8

The Unexpected

"Not everything that is faced can be changed, but nothing can be changed until it is faced."

James Baldwin

Most funerals are uneventful in that there is nothing unusual about them; only the deceased and the family change. With that said, there is the occasional unexpected event that will leave memories for years to come. Some of these happenings may add to the grief, while others provide a time for humor.

Distractions Judged

One such Homegoing service that recently took place at our church was for one of our retired judges. I have attended several funerals of judges over the past two decades. I know that when such a service takes place, a contingent of thirty or more judges show up in their judicial robes. The family had been seated at this particularly lengthy service, followed by the deceased's colleagues – judges all in somber, sedate black robes. What made this procession unusual was the last person in line behind the judges. Dressed in a full Native American headdress was a black man who seemed to be in his late forties. As he approached the casket, he held his headdress to keep it from falling off and bent over to kiss the judge. One of the ministers and the funeral director immediately grabbed hold of him and walked him away to be seated.

Unfortunately, he did not remain seated. He proceeded to walk all around the sanctuary while the service continued. He had told the funeral director and minister, who tried to keep him seated, that he was a family member. That may or may not have been true, but this distraction, undoubtedly made many of the funeral goers assembled uncomfortable. He continued to walk around the entire church. What was his purpose in wearing Native American attire? In this day of strange happenings worldwide, what would he do next? His walking around throughout half of what turned out to be a four-hour service was diverting the congregants' attention from the service. Most families have at least one person who walks to the beat of a different drummer. If indeed he was a member of the judge's family, as he claimed, he may have been the outcast of this family.

As the service continued, the funeral director finally convinced this guy to sit next to him, to which he acquiesced. But his time on that pew did not last long. He got up and went around speaking to members of the family seated on the family pew at the front. All eyes were on him. After shaking a couple of family members' hands, he walked to the back of the church with the funeral director and a couple of security men behind him. As he made his exit from the sanctuary, he let the three who were escorting him out know he felt harassed. If *he* felt harassed, I wonder what the feelings were of the 500+ people in attendance?

After his departure, the rest of the Homegoing service went well, without further distractions.

Seeing Double

I arrived at the services for one of our older members whom I did not know. Once inside the sanctuary, I was taken aback. Instead of one casket at the altar, there were two. Who could this other casket belong to? The obituaries had not been passed out yet by the ushers. These programs are reserved for distribution as the family enters. Another few deacons from our team were assigned to this funeral, and they were just as shocked as I was. There was a significantly smaller crowd in attendance, compared to many of our sanctuary's services. By the time the services got underway, there were fewer than 100 people in attendance for the final remembrances for the lives of two people.

The double obituary was distributed. After reading it, it became apparent that a mother and her daughter were both being funeralized at the same time. What had happened? Only one service had been announced, and now we had two 'dearly departed'? As the story unfolded, the daughter who lived out of state had come to visit her mother, who was gravely ill. While the daughter was here, the mother passed away. It was only a matter of a couple of days, while preparing for her mother's services at the church that she too had died. There were only a few family members who helped prepare for the services. They'd considered having the daughter shipped back to her home state for services, but decided against that expense and chose to have both at the same time and location. Everything was doubled – the obituary had life stories of both mother and daughter, and each had her own eulogy, done by the minister. There was no burial – both bodies were committed before leaving the sanctuary and driven to the crematory for cremation.

Cold Distractions

It was a cold Saturday afternoon in November when I participated in the funeral of a 65-year-old lady whose mother, daughter, and two aunts were members of our congregation. After arriving at the funeral home, which I had never been in before, I sought out the family, whom I did not know. One of the aunts recognized me as a deacon at her church. I introduced myself to the rest of the family and offered condolences on behalf of the pastor and church family. Since I did not know the family, I visited briefly with the mother to make sure our church's Resolution was correct, with the names of all their family members who belonged to our church. A couple of corrections needed to be made to the Resolution, which I made, so the family members were listed correctly.

The funeral was about 15 minutes late getting started, and a funeral home staff member came to the microphone to apologize that there was no heat. He never stated if the cause was furnace failure or failure to pay the heating bill. The temperature outside was about 40°, but inside, even with about 200 people who had kept on their coats, it felt colder than the outside temperature. The minister still had not arrived, neither had the obituary programs to let you know the order of service (the obits finally came close to the end of the service.) During the first 15 minutes or more of the service, the soloist sang two beautiful numbers while the funeral home personnel shared a few more housekeeping points, including silencing all cell phones. It was only a matter of four or five minutes later that someone's phone rang with an obnoxious ringtone. Not only did the phone ring, but the owner put it on speaker, and a voice at the other end said "Hello" in a deep baritone voice. For the first time since entering this funeral parlor, there was a sudden silence for that moment. Was it God calling? Nothing else was heard as the noise of children and adult conversation continued.

Since I was there to read the Resolution and a letter from our senior pastor, I wanted to sit close to the podium, so I wouldn't have to walk in front of the casket. I found a row close enough, where only two people were seated. Moments later, my row was invaded by five small children, ages 3–5, I reckoned. I then looked at the other end. A few people were coming on that side, so there I was, stuck in the middle. Later, I would need to make my way to the aisle when the Acknowledgement time came. As I looked around, I noticed at least 20–25 children. That was highly unusual. The children in my row acted as if they were at recess. They were unruly. They were busy, eating Cheetos, drinking water, talking, and playing … at a funeral! A lady in the row in front of me turned around and told the children, "Be quiet. You're making too much noise. People are trying to listen." A lady seated two chairs to my left yelled back, "Leave my kids alone. Let them talk and play. They're kids!" Because of the tone of this mother's voice, I sat still, not wanting her yelling at me.

By this time, the little 5-year-old girl seated to my right was rubbing her fingers in my gray beard. I softly whispered to her, "Don't do that." I certainly did not want to say anything to her mother after witnessing her outburst to the lady in front of me. After a few minutes, the little girl, stepping on both my shined shoes, went to another row to bother somebody she apparently knew. The service continued, and I was able to read the Resolution and letter shortly after that. The minister had a great eulogy, and the noise level quieted down as he delivered a great message.

Although I didn't know anyone there, I was tempted to leave early, which I consider a no-no after having had a speaking part. After all, it was warmer outside than in the funeral home, and I was cold. One of my biggest pet peeves at a funeral is to see someone who makes any remarks, reads, or sings, then gets up and leaves before the benediction. So, after the eulogy came a review of the deceased, and then the benediction. Now I was free to go and get on with my plans for that evening. When I got to my car, I discovered I was blocked in the parking lot. This is one time I'm glad I did not drive a huge car or large SUV. After a few maneuvers, I could squeeze my way past the other parked cars and head on to my next destination. When I stopped at the first traffic light, I looked in the vanity mirror inside my car's sun visor. What was that orange color on the right side of my gray beard? It dawned on me: the little girl who sat next to me in the funeral home was not only stroking my well-trimmed beard, but using it as a napkin to wipe Cheetos-dust off her fingers.

Funeral Directors

Funeral Directors, as a group, are usually the epitome of well-respected business people. By attending so many services each year, I've gotten to be on a first-name basis with quite a few. The funeral homes that handle services at our church know our protocol – from where to park the hearse as well as all the other parts of the service where they are involved – from start to finish.

On a beautiful summer day as I entered the church for a service, I began to see storm clouds forming. Not literal clouds, but the protocols typically followed were all being ignored. The tension in the air was evident, coming from those who attended as many or more funerals as I had. There was a new funeral home handling this funeral and they insisted on changing everything. The hearse was not parked in the church's drive, as all the hearses and family cars are parked. The three new women funeral directors had the casket in an awkward position at the front of the church, plus, the body in the casket was raised too high, so you saw the body upon entering the sanctuary, instead of seeing it as you are near or at the casket. Our church always brings the family into the sanctuary to view their loved one, and then they are led to the atrium for light refreshments or a meal.

On this day, the new funeral personnel escorted the family right back to the atrium for refreshments without first viewing their loved one. The head director had no problem setting the record straight when told by the officiating minister they were doing everything entirely different than we do in the one hundred plus funerals we have each year. To this, the lady replied, "I don't tell you how to preach your sermons, so don't tell me how to conduct my funerals." Needless to say, that was the first and the last time *that* funeral home has been to our church. I have since wondered if, with that kind of cavalier attitude, if they are still in business.

Some months later, I sat down with one of my good friends, who is a funeral director, to get her input. I was interested in knowing all the different things a funeral director experiences dealing with so many different religious institutions, each with its own customs and traditions of conducting funerals.

Her family celebrated 50 years in the funeral business in 2020, and they had seen many customs, traditions, and changes made during that time. The bottom line is that the role of the funeral director is to serve the needs and wishes of the bereaved family. Most religious institutions seat the family to the right of the casket, but that is not always the case. Most funerals do not open the casket after it's closed at the start of the services, but some reopen it for a parting view. The music played differs. Some allow secular music, others do not. Something we rarely see today is a 'wake,' where family and friends stay up all night with the deceased before the funeral the next day. But if a church or family chooses to do that, is there any reason not to accommodate them?

Most funeral directors follow the protocol of the church and the family's wishes when having the service. My friend told me of a time many years ago when a prominent funeral director in Chicago exercised his intestinal fortitude when he had told the pastor what time they needed to conclude the funeral and be at the cemetery. This funeral had gone long past the deadline to get them to the cemetery, so the funeral director stood up in the back of the church. But the minister continued to preach. The director pointed at his watch. The minister preached on. Finally, he gathered his two attendants, walked down the center aisle, and rolled the casket out of the church to the waiting hearse while the preacher preached on. News of that incident soon got around town. When that funeral home was used from then on, ministers knew when to stop. And they did.

Secret Shared

It was an early afternoon memorial service for the matriarch of a large family. Floral bouquets flanked a picture of this elderly lady in the front of the church. All was going well with the order of service. It had been noted in the obituary program that her body had been donated to science, so there was neither a casket nor an urn with the remains. As the service proceeded, three people gave their remarks, a soloist sang her favorite song, and the Eulogy was given by one of our staff ministers.

However, before the benediction was given, one of the daughters came to the pulpit to share something with everyone present. The family had been told that their mother's body had been donated to science. That was a true statement; the mother had made those arrangements years before her death. However, due to her advanced age and her medical condition at her time of death, her body donation was not accepted. The daughter apologized to the rest of the family for not letting them know. She then informed them that the family's matriarch had been cremated instead. She could not let the family leave the church without letting everyone know the truth.

Sometimes it takes death and then the funeral to get to the truth. To avoid confusion and cause further hurt, it's best to set the record straight about anything in question and bring closure. The Bible validates that when John 8:32 states, *"Then you will know the truth, and the truth will set you free."*

Today donating a body for scientific, medical, or forensic research is typically done through what is called a 'Willed Body Donation Program.' If this is an individual's desire, the family needs to be made aware of donation arrangements. There is no charge to donate, and one can typically donate either designated organs or the whole body. Upon acceptance to donor programs, they usually cover all expenses, including transportation and funeral expenses.

Due to the generosity of those who have donated their body to science in recent years, those of us alive today have benefitted from these gifts through increased life expectancy and increased quality of life. Many medications, orthopedic implants, and numerous other medical advances have been made possible by such donations.

Father's Grief

I have found that funerals for shooting victims are among the most difficult. Too many young people have not had time to live life due to gun violence. Many shootings today seem to be gang related. This one had its origin from a drive-by shooting when an innocent out-of-state college student, who attended our church on Sundays, was killed. He was not the intended target of these gangbangers, but bullets have no eyes, and he became the innocent victim of this senseless crime.

Several police cars were stationed outside the church that day, with several officers inside watching the crowd. As the family was escorted in to view the body, something took place I had not seen before. The parents, who belonged to a church in another state, were led to the casket. The father began to cry loudly. Instead of heading to our atrium for refreshments, he remained in the sanctuary on the pew in front of his son, who lay in the casket, still sobbing and crying. His mourning with the loud sobs and cries lasted the entire two hours while the visitation and service took place.

At the conclusion of the service, a meeting was held in a section of the sanctuary for gang members and others who wanted to talk about ways of helping to end gang violence. I don't know the outcome of this meeting, but this father and family, could only have wished that that meeting had been held before their son became a victim. Things may have turned out differently.

You may ask, "Where is the good grief or the lighter side in this situation?" Certainly, losing a young person or any other loved one to violence is one of the most hurting types of grief. Today in our country, we lose far too many loved ones in this manner. Instead of just having a repast that day, family members, gang members, and other young people met to talk about ways they could help thwart violence of this sort. No one person has the answer, but if we all band together to address the issue and speak out when needed, maybe, just maybe, we might affect a considerable decrease in gun violence in our cities.

Family Drama

Let's face up to it – funerals can bring much family drama. We all know this should not be the place to resolve conflict, but it happens in family after family. I personally have witnessed situations that were not only embarrassing or humorous, but many leave a lasting impression that dishonors the life of the deceased.

This conflict can be seen in many different forms. I have been to two funerals in recent years where both the widows of the deceased and mistresses were in attendance and grieving. At one funeral, the mistress got up and paid tribute to the man with whom she'd had a long-lasting affair. You can only imagine the eyebrows that were raised, as well as the whispers that went on.

In the second one, the widow was so overcome with grief that she jumped from her seat, shouted, and snatched the wig off the mistress sitting a few rows behind her. That fight might still be going on had not some attendees gotten up to break it up between the two of them.

A third one, shared with me by a prison ministry partner, involved the funeral of her own daughter's estranged husband who had died while living with another woman. Both sides of the two families had considerably different plans for the funeral services, so much so that armed police officers were present to keep the peace between the two families.

Not only does family drama take place at a funeral, but it may also continue for some time. I'm reminded of the story of a man who went to the cemetery to visit the grave of a loved one. While there, he could not help but hear a man sobbing loudly at a nearby fresh grave. Between sobs, the man beat the ground and wailed, "Why did you have to die? Why did you have to die!" Thinking he might be able to offer some solace, this man went over to the sobbing gentleman and said, "I'm so sorry to hear you're grieving so much. You evidently were quite close to the departed." The sobbing man stopped weeping long enough to say, "No, I never knew him, but I married his widow."

How can we mitigate the conflict that often occurs among relatives at a funeral? Perhaps the following suggestions can be employed during a funeral to diffuse family tensions:

Show Respect

Regardless of whether you respect the actions of family members or not, you are all grieving. Everyone deserves the time to mourn. You may disagree with what may be going on, decisions made, money issues, attitudes, and a plethora of emotions, but now is not the time to publicly display your thoughts and feelings. Don't forget, you're family by blood or marriage, and you're all in this together. Validate the grief of others in your family, and don't cause drama.

Printed Obituaries

What is written about the deceased and next of kin in the newspaper, social media, or on a printed program at the funeral can lead to irritations. Everything from, who the survivors are, name spellings, who was omitted, etc., can leave hurt feelings and outbursts. I even recall one funeral where obituary programs were passed out in the church before the services. After the funeral was over, another side of the family distributed completely different obituary programs outside in the parking lot.

Please Behave

It should not have to be said that everyone should be on their best behavior on the day of a family funeral. Needless to say, that does not always happen. You cannot control how others act, but you can control your reactions. Be kind and avoid confrontation as much as possible. Do not bring up topics that you know to be contentious and may fuel the fire.

Final Gathering

After the funeral is over and it's time for the repast, dinner, or social gathering, a lot of conversation usually occurs about the day. Regardless of what someone said, what somebody wore, who was with whom, or other trivial conversation that may take place, now is not the time to get involved in this chatter. Stay low-key, and allow your loved one's day not to be tarnished but honored.

Left Behind

Mourning takes place at all funerals in some aspect. The reason behind the tears and other displays of grief is not always evident. I have generally found that, in many cases, those who cry the most do so because they could not make peace with the loved one before death. Or perhaps, the guilt of doing the least for that person before they died. I've seen people almost try to get into the casket before it's closed. I've also occasionally witnessed a mourner passing out. Many of these emotions and more can be expected in occasional situations from time to time. I have also come to realize there are quite a few who mourn over the *stuff* left behind by the deceased. I have on many occasions heard, "I wonder how much they left." The answer to that question is quite simple – they left it all. I have yet to see a funeral procession with an armored vehicle or moving van behind the hearse. Just as sure as we came into this world with nothing, we will leave the same way. Far too many grieve over what they may not receive of the deceased's material wealth. Some of those have mourned that they were left out of the will. Others argue they should have been the recipient of the car, the china, the furs, the jewelry, the money ... and the list goes on and on. Families are often divided and argue over the disposition of the assets and may not speak to each other for years to come.

Settling the estate and deciding what to do with years of accumulated belongings of your loved one is a task. Anyone who has moved knows the work involved in moving. This task is just as daunting, if not more so. The disposition of everything left behind usually falls into one of four categories: *Donate, Keep, Sell, or Trash*. Determine who will make these decisions. Then it's time to get started. Plan the days and times you will be sorting through the years or decades of memories left behind. Decide who among family and friends you will want to help you. Plan the order in which you want to go through all the things. Many find it easier to go room by room, boxing, and labeling, but do what works best for you. The whole process can be overwhelming, but don't rush it. On the other hand, don't procrastinate; it must be done sooner rather than later.

Words Expressed

Most people mean no harm when they speak to the family, but the awkward or inappropriate words that come from the mouths of those wishing to console can often hurt more than help. Through the years of hundreds of funerals, I have heard words spoken to the family and others, that would have been better left unspoken. Going back to the TV show from years ago with Art Linkletter (and others in more recent years) called *Kids Say the Darndest Things*, the same is true of words spoken during a family's time of bereavement. The following are just some of the things I have heard others say or have been shared with me:

"How did he die?" Although many may think those thoughts, they should never be spoken. If the family wants to voice the cause of death, let them do so. You don't need to bring it up.

"Your loved one doesn't look like him/herself in that casket." We have no idea what has changed their appearance from how we remembered them. I recall a good friend whose head was three times bigger in his casket than when alive. And another who had been dead for several days before she was discovered was only recognizable by her distinct nose shape that had not changed. The family knows their loved one does not look as they did before death, and there's no need for us to

bring it to their attention. In some instances, the family may need to have a closed casket, so this question is not raised.

"Why did you have that dress put on her? The color is not right for her." Believe me when I say I have seen bodies adorned in all sorts of attire, most are appropriate, but some make you think, why that outfit? Just don't comment on the apparel that doesn't seem to become the deceased.

"Will you have the watch, glasses, and jewelry removed before burial? After all, there's no need to have those items buried too." Maybe it was per the deceased's request to have those items in the casket. Perhaps the family thought it might enhance the viewing. Whatever the reason, the family has decided, and it's not our place to question their choices.

"He or she is in a better place now." Unless you have been to that better place, how do you know? Sometimes this statement can cause pain to a grieving person and fuel religious arguments. It may be true if the deceased suffered a long and painful illness preceding death, but this statement often gets mixed reactions.

"You're strong enough to handle this." Or, *"The Lord doesn't give us burdens we can't handle."* There is nothing like adding more pressure to a person who is already weakened during this time of bereavement. Most grieving people need to have the support and strength of family and friends to get through this period until well after the funeral is over.

"I know what you're going through." You may have suffered the loss of a loved one close to you, but each individual's experience is different. All relationships are unique, with varying dynamics. We cannot say we understand what that person is truly feeling.

"Did he or she have life insurance?" I have heard this insensitive question addressed to a grieving family on more than one occasion. During a family's time of bereavement or at the visitation or funeral is not the time for you to pry into their financial affairs. If you wish to donate to

the family, please leave it with them in a sympathy card, or mail it to them. Asking this question is certainly not necessary.

"I know you're lonely, but you will find a new spouse." To the widow or widower, their mind is only on the one they have spent years of their life with. Thinking about replacing that person usually is the farthest thing from their mind currently.

"How does it feel being a widow?" These were the words a widow from my church was asked just months after burying her husband. She knew the lady who asked her at church by face only. Not until then did the realism of those words hit her and bring back a wave of grief all over again.

Instead of saying the 'wrong things' to those grieving, first try listening. Don't push your agenda by waving your magic wand to make it all go away. In other words, don't try to fix it. Forget about using worn-out clichés and just be honest. Too many times we try to say the right thing and fail. It's all right not to say anything, but just to give a hug or handshake. The most effective expressions are your ministry of presence and simple and quiet support.

Thoughts to ponder: Do you remember a time during the passing of a loved one when things didn't go as expected? If yes, have you moved on from that time or asked for strength to put the incident in your past? What can you do to minimize family bickering over material possessions left by your loved one?

Chapter 9

Seasonal Sadness

To everything there is a season and a time to every purpose under the heaven.

Ecclesiastes 3:1

Every February, my wife has a few melancholy moments. This is the month she remembers three significant people in her life who either had a birthday, died, or became missing in that month. She remembers the birthday of the mother who raised her, the death of her first husband, and a brother who disappeared and was never found.

To a close friend of mine, October is that time of the year she remembers the deaths of several family members close to her. I have a friend who tears up every time she smells the fragrance her late husband once wore.

Another friend, whose mother passed in 2011, is reminded of her every time he goes to a particular Chinatown bakery. He buys these small egg custard pies that remind him of the egg custard pies his mother baked when he was growing up in Alabama.

Yet, for many friends and family, specific dates such as birthdays, anniversaries, dates of death, and funeral dates start tears flowing or bring back memories that may leave the individual in a somewhat depressed state of mind. These times of sadness are real and can take years to diminish if they ever do.

Remembrance Services

Every December, our church has a Service of Remembrance to which families who have lost loved ones recently are invited. It is usually held on a Saturday or Sunday afternoon in our sanctuary. It follows a regular order of church service, even with a sermon to comfort the bereaved. Other churches and some funeral homes offer a similar service. Each person is given a light to activate at the conclusion of the service, as they leave the sanctuary and proceed to our Atrium area. There, another memorial offering will take place. Each person receives a paper star with an ornament hook for members of their family they wish to write their names on and hang on one of a pair of Christmas trees to honor that loved one's memory. The ceremony closes with a prayer, and those in attendance can stay as long as they desire for refreshments and fellowship.

Coping Strategies

The time between Thanksgiving and New Year's is especially a time of seasonal sadness for many. Holiday cheer eludes some who are grieving. Many have lost loved ones during this time of the year, and each holiday season reopens those memories anew.

Allow me to offer some tips for coping with seasonal sadness, regardless of the time of year that sadness may come to you.

1. *Allow yourself time and space to process your emotions.*

When death comes, we all experience periods of suffering from our loss. Some take longer than others to heal. Realize it is okay not to feel like you usually do. Be patient with yourself. Allow conversations with family and friends, events you attend, and other personal activities to help you reconnect with your emotional side.

2. *Focus on activities that fulfill you.*

Take part in things you may not have been involved in when your loved one was still alive. It could be taking classes that may interest you, spending time at the gym, and doing some things that may have been unfamiliar to you before your loved one passed. This is a time to reflect on meeting your own needs and finding new events, activities, and friends who can bring new meaning to your life.

3. *Seek professional help, grief resources.*

Don't go it alone. Do not be embarrassed to let others know you feel lonely or depressed. Be proactive in seeking professional guidance if family and friends are not helping you get through this period. Outside help and grief support groups can help you see brighter days ahead.

4. *Connect with friends and family.*

Having a support system of family and friends during periods of seasonal sadness is essential. Call up and get together with those friends who know what you're going through when those times of sorrow hit you in ways you may not have expected. Those few people can be your lifeline to getting you back to where you need and want to be.

5. Practice self-care.

Self-care is essential daily, but even more so when you are grieving. You need to get plenty of rest, watch your diet, and do things that will help you physically and emotionally during this time. Get out and about as you are able and avoid spending too much time alone and thinking about what keeps you out of sorts and depressed.

6. Go to events you will feel comfortable attending.

You may want to pace yourself and accept invitations to events and gatherings where you feel comfortable. It's okay to say no to some activities that may remind you of the time you spent doing them with your loved one.

7. Try new things.

Perhaps your family always did the same things around the holidays. Try starting anything new that will put you in a different state of mind. Change is good, especially if it requires you to look at things not connected to recent memories that were always there.

8. Travel somewhere if possible.

Travel is an excellent way for many to escape and discover new things and places. Whether it is around the holidays, or any other time of the year, when you lost that loved one, take time to see new places and get a new outlook.

9. Keep a daily journal.

Writing in a journal each day can help you get through some of these times. It can help you also see the progress you have made year after year. A therapist I know gives assignments to her patients to keep a gratitude journal. They are asked to write down at least one thing for which they are grateful every day. She states research shows it even rewires the brain for happiness.

10. Create your own celebration.

When those days come that bring sadness your way, instead of staying home and dwelling on your sorrow, create ways to share and celebrate with others so that you are not alone.

11. Spend time in meditation and prayer.

First and foremost, spend time in meditation and prayer. These two daily practices will help you draw upon the strength you need to make it through these times of sadness. Instead of making every effort to run away from sadness, deliberately spend some time remembering happy times with the departed loved one, either alone or with family members or close friends.

During the pandemic of 2020–21, our Trinity UCC Emmaus Road Grief Support ministry met once or twice a month via zoom. Due to the pandemic, zoom video sessions had become a way of life. I found myself in 6–8 zoom sessions each week. The zoom sessions for me ran the gamut from family/personal, numerous church ministries/committee meetings, homeowner association meetings, etcetera. At one point, I told my wife I am getting zoomed out. I want to see real people and not just 'zoom people.'

For many weeks, my brother Lawrence had been texting me weekly spiritual messages from a minister in Georgia who visits their church in Indiana each Fall. One week I received a text message dealing with grief. It was just in time for our Emmaus Road Grief Support Ministry meeting. The homework assignment for all who had been present during the prior session was to share suggestions for coping with grief. As we opened our session that evening, I shared the text message I had been forwarded with the group. The message was timely as I read to those on my computer screen the following:

The company of MANY does not erase the loss of one. Grief is not a DISORDER, DISEASE, nor a sign of WEAKNESS. Grief is an emotional, physical, and spiritual NECESSITY, the price you pay for LOVE. The only cure for GRIEF is to GRIEVE. We cannot say God always fills our EMPTINESS caused by the loss of our loved ones. God sometimes leaves it unfilled but helps us persevere, even in pain. The more beautiful and fuller our remembrances are, the more difficult the separation, but the GRATITUDE transforms the TORMENT of memory into SILENT JOY!!

That statement set the tone that night for the dozen or more who signed on to our session via their phone, tablet, or computer. Everyone had coping strategies they shared, allowing each person to note a plethora of ways to deal with their grief. At the end of that session, a phone number to the Compassion Helpline was placed in the chat box for anyone who felt the need to call and talk with a counselor for further coping support.

Thoughts to ponder: What coping strategies are you using to get you through those periods of seasonal sadness you may still experience?

Chapter 10

The Burial

O death, where is thy sting? O grave, where is thy victory?

I Corinthians 15:55

After Sherri and I had been married, we had a humorous disagreement that went on for many years. She had already made her decision to be cremated. I, for a fact, knew I did not like heat, and, most certainly, being cremated was not something I wanted my body to go through, even after death. As I continued to be indecisive about my means of disposal upon my death, Sherri would remind me if I didn't decide before I passed away, she would put me in a trash bag and bury me in the backyard or have me interred alongside her first husband in the cemetery in which he was buried. Given those two options, I finally chose to be cremated, which I learned is a much more economical and practical choice. Also, being cremated will allow my immediate family to have parts of my cremains encased in jewelry or placed in an urn if they so choose. The odds of my family coming to visit me at a cemetery, I thought, would be slim-to-none, so why take up that space?

It took almost 20 years of marriage to make that final decision. At least I've decided before my wife had to do that for me.

Today, commonly practiced legal methods include in-ground burial, unless you are interred in an area below sea level, like New Orleans, where above-ground burial is necessary. Other methods include cremation, entombment in an above-ground mausoleum, burial at sea, and dissolution, which involves breaking down the body in an acid solution, then disposing of the liquid.

Late Arrival

Although I have been to many funerals, being a part of a funeral procession headed to a cemetery has been minimal. Unless the burial was a member of my own family, or I served as a pallbearer, or was extremely close to the family – as the service at the church or funeral home ended, so would my involvement. The same has been true with the repast that follows the burial. I only attend those dinners if I have been at the interment.

One service my wife and I attended that involved my presence from start to finish was for one of my wife's relatives in Youngstown, Ohio. We arrived in Youngstown the night before the funeral and stayed at a hotel. The weather was unseasonably hot for late June. The following morning, we checked out of the hotel and joined the rest of the family at the home of the relative, from which the funeral procession would leave, headed to the church. The church was packed this Saturday morning. Although the minister who was officiating tried to move the services along to arrive at the cemetery on time, his efforts were less than successful. Trying to rush those who were part of the processional to the final resting place was almost like herding cats. On Saturdays, this cemetery closed at 1:00 p.m. The procession, however, arrived ten or fifteen minutes late. Normally, for the graveside committal, chairs and a canopy are provided at the gravesite. But when the procession came to a stop by the side of the road, only an open grave with six gravediggers and a truckload of dirt greeted us. Instead of the pallbearers taking the casket from the hearse to the gravesite, the minister committed the body by the roadside, prayed, and ended with the traditional "earth to earth, ashes to ashes, and dust to dust" committal. As soon as he was done, the six gravediggers rushed the casket to the open grave, lowered it down, put the vault top on the casket, and the dump truck filled with dirt from the freshly dug grave, refilled it while close to 150 people watched in awe.

What was the rationale for this hastiness? Being late to the cemetery was the answer. There were two options the family had; either take the body back to the funeral home and return on Monday for a proper committal … and pay an extra charge, or have it done in the manner the family had just witnessed. I believe the cost and inconvenience drove that decision.

Military Burial

On numerous occasions, I have been to the funeral of a deceased who has served in the military. But I've seldom been to a national cemetery where the burial took place. The first national cemetery I recall going to was in Dayton, Ohio. It was the graveside committal after the funeral for my Uncle Alex back in the '70s. The 21-gun salute and the mournful rendition of Taps on the bugle give one a sense of the respect we have for those who have served in the military.

The other most memorable military service I remember took place in the Chicagoland area. The father of one of our members had passed, and a longtime friend of the son wanted to attend. His only challenge was that public transportation did not extend to this far south suburban community where the funeral was held. My friend, who had served in our prison ministry, asked if he could ride with me to the service. I agreed to drive downtown to pick him up on the morning of the funeral. It was not out of my way because I needed to drop off my granddaughter at a program downtown.

I picked my friend Anthony up from his train stop, and we drove for nearly an hour to get to the church in the south suburb where the visitation started at 10:00 and the funeral at 11:00. Everything went very smoothly, and the services concluded at about Noon. I thought I had plenty of time to get my friend back downtown and wait for my granddaughter's program to end so I could take her home. However, my friend decided he wanted to go to the interment at Abraham Lincoln National Cemetery in Elwood, Illinois. I had not been there before and thought, oh well, this shouldn't take that long. I thought I might be cutting it close, but I could still pick up my granddaughter on schedule at 3:00. Was I in for a shock! It took us an hour to get to the cemetery, and when we arrived shortly after 1:00, we had to wait at the entrance. I began to count the other funeral processions that followed us: a total of six. Although we were the first to arrive, each had a scheduled time. We learned that this ceremony with the firing of three volleys from rifles would be at 2:45 pm. There was no way I could pick my granddaughter up on time, even if I had a helicopter, which I did not. I called my wife, working from home, to share my dilemma. Fortunately, she was able to drive downtown to get our granddaughter.

Meanwhile, back at the national cemetery, the 2:45 p.m. time for this graveside tribute arrived on that cold and cloudy late fall afternoon. The rifle salute, folding of the flag that had draped the casket, its presentation to the family, and blowing of Taps was just as I had remembered from years past. By now it was shortly after 3:00, and my friend Anthony was hungry. He asked if we could go back to the church where dinner was served. Since we had come this far, I decided we might as well head back to the church and eat the meal that was already prepared.

The drive back to the church was shorter that time since we were not in a funeral procession driving 35 mph. We got back around 3:45 p.m. Around 4:30, they finally began to serve all those who hung out to the end. When we finished, I drove my fellow prison ministry friend back to the end of the 'red line' L Station so he could take the train home. I finally made it home a little before 7:00 p.m. What a long day!

It had been almost twelve hours since I left home that morning. If all the funerals I attended took that much time out of my day, needless to say, I would be attending far fewer of them. Not only was that my first time at that national cemetery in Elwood, but it will probably be my last if I have a say in the matter.

Double Wide

There have been a few times over the years when I have served as a pallbearer. Most funerals have six pallbearers who assist the funeral home personnel in taking the casket from the church or funeral home to the cemetery if burial is the final part of the service. One of the first funerals that I served in this capacity was for a dear friend in Kansas City who passed away at well over 400 pounds. I had never given much thought to the problems obesity has caused in our country until this funeral. The National Center for Health Statistics estimates that 39.8% of adults aged 20 and over are obese, with 7.6% of those severely obese.

Services for my friend Harold were held at a funeral home. It was a cold and snowy day in late January, the kind of day you stay home unless it's vital to leave. It took me twice as long to drive to the services as I imagine it did for the other people who braved the inclement weather. The attendance was lower than it may have been due to the weather, but a hundred or so brave souls were there to support this family.

After the services were over, it felt as if it took everyone in the funeral home parking lot as long to get their cars cleaned off as it did for the funeral service itself. I recall the struggle it took for eight men to carry this oversized coffin from the funeral home to the waiting hearse. Little did I imagine *this* would be the easy part. It took what seemed to be an eternity for the procession to get to the cemetery due to the icy, snow-packed streets. Once the procession of some twenty cars arrived, we pallbearers were asked to leave our cars to help the funeral director take the casket to the waiting gravesite, that was sheltered by a canopy. The distance from the road, where the hearse was parked, to the gravesite was several hundred feet. With every step of the way, carrying this heavy casket, I kept asking myself, "Are we there yet?" By the time we almost got the casket to the open grave, one of the older pallbearers tripped and fell, necessitating the other seven of us to hold his portion until he was back on his feet. By now, all of us assembled for the committal were in a hurry for things to end so we could return to a warmer and dryer place.

I have not been to many funerals with oversized caskets, but for sure, as I continue to live, I know there will be some in my future. I don't believe from now on, I shall have the stamina to serve as a pallbearer at a funeral with an oversized casket. For those younger men I would say, stay strong and be prepared. Furthermore, for anyone who is a candidate for one of these caskets I would say – not only is it longer and deeper than a regular casket, but it will also cost the family any amount up from $2,500 to purchase. That does not include the extra cost in grave plots should the deceased be buried, plus transportation, and the lifting equipment that may enter the picture.

Needless to say, many of us will not change our lifestyles. Obesity is not only hazardous to our own physical health, but can also be a heavy burden on our family's financial health as well. Not to mention those who must physically carry the deceased to a final resting place.

Thoughts to ponder: Whether it is a serene outdoor setting, cremation, or enclosed mausoleum, what have you chosen for your final resting place that can reflect your life story? Have you made pre-arrangements, so your family has one less worry when you pass away?

The Epilogue

"The two most important days in your life are the day you are born and the day you find out why."

Mark Twain

If death is one of the greatest mysteries in life, then life itself must be just as mystifying. We have explored many aspects of grief and mourning in this book. Now it is time to put it all into perspective. Biblically speaking, our purpose in life is to do everything for the glory of God (1Corinthians 10:13). Hopefully, you have been fulfilling that purpose. But if not, allow the writer of Ecclesiastes to summarize it for us. In the 3rd chapter, verses 1-8, he writes:

To everything there is a season, and a time to every purpose under the Heaven: A time to be born, and a time to die; a time to plant, and a time to pluck up that which is planted; A time to kill, and a time to heal; a time to break down and a time to build up; a time to weep and a time to laugh; a time to mourn and a time to dance; a time to cast away stones, and a time to gather stones together; a time to embrace, and a time to refrain from embracing; a time to get, and a time to lose; a time to keep and a time to cast away; a time to rend, and a time to sew; a time to keep silence, and a time to speak; a time to love, and a time to hate; a time of war, and a time of peace.

Let's take a look into the future. Suddenly, everything goes dark. Then it appears we are in a dream. We see people, many of whom we know. They are all gathered and mingling in a large gathering place. We smell flowers, hear music softly playing in the background and see created Birthday, Anniversary, Thank You, and Get-Well greeting cards displayed with pictures of many different people inside them. Could it be that we're at a funeral? After what appears to be about an hour, the music ends, and a voice at the podium announces, "Will everyone be seated as the family enters the sanctuary?" At that moment, we see a familiar family all processing towards a casket surrounded by flowers. It turns out that the voice is that of a minister we know, reciting scripture while soft music has resumed. Once the family has made its way in and been seated, the minister welcomes everyone to this Homegoing service.

"But whose service is it, we ask?" We do not have a copy of the obituary, but everyone else appears to have one. The minister gives the opening invocation followed by a familiar opening hymn led by the choir. Once the hymn is over, two scriptures are read, the first from the Old Testament, followed by one from the New Testament. Everyone is asked to be seated while the choir sings one of the deceased's favorite songs. Following the song that leaves tears in the eyes of many, three people who knew the deceased well are asked to give their tributes. The first speaker represents the neighborhood and community where the deceased lived; the second, the religious institution of which this person was an active member. Finally, the third to take the microphone is a member of the deceased's family. All three speakers had great memories to share about the life of the one lying before them in the casket. All these things have taken place up to this point, but the individual's name in the casket is never mentioned. "Why don't those with speaking parts just say the name, so we know whose life we are honoring?" we think to ourselves.

The next part of the service involves reading several Resolutions from organizations to which the deceased belonged. Even after these several moments go by, we still have no mention of a name to give us a clue.

Now the clergy is back before the microphone and asks everyone to read the obituary silently while the music softly plays. Since we do not have an obituary program, we still are in the dark about who has died. Acknowledgements are then made, and next, the voices we hear are the choir as they render yet another song the deceased loved dearly. After the song is over, the minister approaches the podium to offer Words of Comfort. We guess, now we will find out whose life we are celebrating.

The minister delivers a prayer as he begins to celebrate a life well-lived. He takes a scripture from the Bible and gives a title to his message. For about twenty or twenty-five minutes, he orates excellent things accomplished in the life of the one who lies in the casket. He shares stories about many memorable moments experienced by the dearly departed. A Biblical application about the deceased's life is made from the scripture lesson read, but still no mention of the name. As the minister closes out his sermon, everyone is on their feet, giving applause to such a great oration. As the crowd remains standing, he calls the funeral directors to the front of the church so the flowers can be taken out preceding the casket. But wait, we have witnessed this whole funeral, and we still do not know whose life and legacy we just concluded. At that moment, something out of the ordinary happens.

A final review is allowed by request of the family. Mourner after mourner files by the casket that is now open to pay their last respects. As the last person in the sanctuary passes by, we too are allowed to take a final view. As we approach the casket, no corpse is seen from a distance. As we finally get to the casket and look from a few feet away, we are in shock. There's no body in the casket! What was this funeral all about? Where is the body of the person whose life we were celebrating? A few more steps, and we're looking down inside a casket where a mirror rests. We look in the mirror, and we see ourselves. All of a sudden, there's silence. Yes, this was our day to be celebrated. All the years of our life flash before us in the next few moments. Are we satisfied? Are there still questions we have about the life we have lived? Will we be remembered in the years to come? What legacy have we left now that our life is over?

Who will think of us after we have passed away when they read the following poem?

The Moment That You Died
Unknown

The moment that you died, my heart was torn in two,
One side filled with heartache, the other died with you.
I often lie awake at night, when the world is fast asleep,
and take a walk down memory lane, with tears upon my cheeks.
Remembering you is easy, I do it every day,
But missing you is a heartache that never goes away.
I hold you tight within my heart and there you will remain,
Until the joyous day arrives when we shall meet again.

Our life is over. What has been done cannot be undone.

Is there anything we need to do differently before that time comes? Now is the time to put our house in order. We may mourn over someone else who has recently passed. Someday others may mourn because of the life we have lived. Let our life be one that will bring good grief.

Patrons

A heartfelt thank you to the Patrons who helped make this book a reality. Thank you for your advance purchase of this publication, months before it was produced.

Sincerely,

Ed

Bryant	Alexander
Doris	Allen
Eleanor	Anderson
Wacile	Anderson
Brandon	Avery
Diane	Baker
Angela	Baker-Brown
Ellen C.	Barnes
Diana	Beasley
Bob & Donna	Bednar
Mike & Lauretta	Bentz
Christine	Berzins
Cynthia T.	Blackwood
Sharon	Blaine
Don & Judy	Blanton
Ed & Lorraine	Bowman

Danita	Brown
Fred & Charnett	Brown
Norval I Brown &	Andrea L. Brookins
Walter	Brown
Randall & Regena	Caldwell
David M.	Carter
Luesther	Chapman
Thurman & Cleopatra	Chisholm
Doretha	Clark
Gerald & Paulette	Clinkscales, Sr.
Charles & Carole	Cobb
Donald	Coleman
Deneen	Collins
Nonnie	Conner
Carlos & Odessia Spruill	Corniffe
Noreen	Costelloe
Janice	Crayton
Bob & Cathy	Dale
Anthony & Georgette	Davis
William & Heather	Davis
Steve & Nancy	Dean
Sherry	Dockery
Bill & Diana	Ducett
Linda B.	Echols
Maurice	Ellis
Dyanne	Elzia
Deacon Dion & Sharon	Fleming
Deborah	Fletcher
Darlene	Flynn
Charisse	Franklin
Henry & Jiles	George

Evelyn	Gooden
Pamela J.	Goodman
Rupert & Karen	Graham
Gail	Hardy
Carmen L.	Harley
George & Damita	Harrell
Corrine	Harris
Ed & Mary	Harrison
Michael	Heard
Terrylon & Deborah	Higgins
Anthony M.	Hill, III
Jasmyn Lee	Hinton
Lee & Charlotte	Holloway
Hydie	Hoskins
Lynda A.	Hughes
Leslie & Diana	Hughey
April	Janney
Jack	Johnson
Letitia I	Johnson
Mr. & Mrs Philip & Cassandra	Johnson, Sr
Richard & Laura	Johnson
Rev. Calvon	Jones
Robert & Renier	Jones
Craig J.	Kurth, CFP
Mike	Lebarre
Barbara	Little
Pamela	Love
Patricia	Love
Chuck & Bonita	Maclin
Leroy & Rosemary	Marshall
Adrianne (AJ)	Mason

Dorothy L.	Mason
Lawrence & Vanessa	Mason
Sharon	Matthews
Rev. Cedric L. & Dr. Michele	McCay
Eva Mae	McDaniels-Brown
Michele	McGee
Billy & Derrell	McGhee
Marian	McKinney
Deborah Turner	McKissic
Janet L.	Merrills
Eugene	Miller
Rev. Dr. & Mrs. Michael	Miller, Sr.
Daniel & Ludeen	Moore
Melody	Morgan
Mr. & Mrs. Archester	Neal
Mr. & Mrs. Fulton & Deborah	Nolen, Jr.
Linda	Owens
Charles & Erica	Perry
Drs. Lamorris & Carmella	Perry
Jacqueline	Perry
Richard & Delores	Piehl
Junior & Tanika	Pierre
Austin & Rhonda	Pope
Colleen	Porter
Nicholas	Porter
Deacon Vincent & Aretha	Price
Rosalyn	Priester
Sandra H.	Quick
Adah Marie	Roberts
Lisa	Roberts
Zelza	Roberts

Eddie & Alice	Rollins
Angelo & Galyin	Rose
Karl	Ross
Edward & Mae Sue	Rule
Charles	Sanders
Dr. Joe & Lisa	Sangster, MD
Rose E.	Scott
Richard & Iris	Sewell
Karen	Simmons
John & Minister Aris	Simpson
Mike & Cheryl	Sledge
Freddye	Smith
Ralph	Smith
Steve & Jackie	Smith
Karl	Sokol
James & Regina	Spiller
Dr. Amelia J.	Stevens
Letitia	Sykes-Matthews
Carol	Taylor
Wynetta	Thomas
Melvin & Briget Woods	Thompson
Elois	Tinsley-Anderson
Carolyn	Triano Rhodes
Phyllis	Tyler
Richard & Gwendolyn	Vaughn
Darryl & Kurnita	Wallace
Minister Attorney Renita	Ward
Vameca	Wheeler
Bernadine	White
Mary	Wilkes
Dr. Constance Y.	Williams

Michelle	Williams
Rebecca	Williamson
Rev. Charlene	Wordlaw-Porter
Dr. Arlethia L.	Wright
Dr. Chloe Ayesha Marie	Wright
Renee Victoria	Wright
Victor & Carrie M.	Wynn
Darwin	Yarborough
Denise	Young

www.ingramcontent.com/pod-product-compliance
Lightning Source LLC
LaVergne TN
LVHW020443070526
838199LV00063B/4837